My Spiritual Journey

An Autobiography by

Rabbi Avraham B. Hecht

Brooklyn, New York

5766 • 2006

My Spiritual Journey

Published and Copyrighted © 2006

by

RABBI ABRAHAM B. HECHT

866 Eastern Parkway / Brooklyn, New York 11213

ISBN 1-884535-07-0

Manufactured in the United States of America

Empire Press Co.

550 Empire Blvd. • Brooklyn, N.Y. 11225 • (718) 756-1473 / Fax (718) 604-7633

This book is dedicated to my dear wife,
partner in life for 59 years
Lieba bas Miriam V'Boruch Greenhut
of blessed memory.
It was her continued support and inspiration that
made my achievements possible.
May her memory be an example
and an inspiration to all of us.

רחמנא ליבא בעי

Introduction

When my Zeide arrived in America, he did not succumb to the prevailing pressures to Americanize. Instead, my Zeide set out to transform the rich but superficial Gashmius of America into the rich and significant Ruchnius of Judaism and Chassidus.

In the merit of my noble grandparents and parents, I have witnessed the Hecht family tradition of uncompromising loyalty to Torah and Mitzvos, all the way from the generosity and humility imbedded in the welcoming warmth of my Grandparent's home, to the excitement and dedication at the Siddur parties and Bar Mitzvah Maamarim of my great-grandchildren. Seven generations!

It is to the younger generations that I dedicate this book. It is my hope and prayer that they will continue to practice, to teach and to inspire countless hundreds and thousands in their important positions in their respective communities, as they serve their Creator according to the teachings of the Lubavitcher Rebbe(s), o.b.m.

I pray that the holy light of Torah and Chassidus continue to glow and warm their hearts and minds to inspire them to attain greater spiritual development and share their lofty traditions with our holy people, Israel.

My prayers will continue unabated, now and in the future, may it be with Moshiach, speedily in our days.

TABLE OF CONTENTS

Foreign Shores

ore than a century after its inception, America of 1885 was an established, expanding country. Citizens running the gamut of all ethnicities and religions tried to disregard their various differences and maintain the peace borne of liberty and freedom.

Into this picture of diversity and acceptance stepped a vivacious young man in his early twenties. His outer appearance sparked the interest of those who caught a glimpse of his aristocratic bearing and unusual garb. My grandfather, R' Tzvi Elimelech Hecht, known as Hersh Meilich, an ardent chassid of the Shinever Rav (son of the Zanser Rebbe — the Divrei Chaim), had reached American shores.

The popular misconception of America as a land which precludes religious observance was widely accepted by the European communities. Thus, it was extremely rare to receive the permission and blessings of a Chassidic Rebbe, to cross the Atlantic. My Zeide, R' Hersh Meilich, was one of the few people to whom permission was granted. Well-acquainted with my grandfather's piety and stringent Torah observance, R' Yecheskel Halberstam, the Shinever Rav, harbored no hesitations concerning the journey.

News of R' Hersh Meilich's imminent departure swept the town in Galicia like stormy ocean waves. Feelings of excitement and fear of the unknown mingled within the hearts of the Chassidic community as they prepared to send off one of their re-vered members.

The wife of the presiding shochet figured that my grandfa-ther's planned emigration set an example for her family as well. This would be the perfect opportunity to undertake the arduous journey to the United States. To her chagrin, the Shinever Rav thought otherwise.

"If you allowed R' Hersh Meilich Hecht to leave, why don't you allow my husband?" she inquired in confusion.

The Rebbe's reply answered her question and highlighted the high regard in which my grandfather was held.

"I can trust R' Hersh Meilich Hecht to remain loyal to his tra-dition, even in adverse religious conditions, but I cannot vouch that your husband will be able to turn away from the many ob-stacles and remain a religious Jew."

Before R' Hersh Meilich parted from his hometown, from the thriving Jewish community and from every aspect of comfortable routine, the Shinever Rav charged him with an important mission to be carried out in the distant land of promise. Placing a push-ka, a collection box, in the hand of his pious chassid, the Rebbe implored him to remember the plight of the poor, indigent Rebbes of Galicia and Poland. Throughout his forays in the New World, he should constantly seek to improve their lot by gather-ing funds for the righteous leaders of the European communi-ties.

My grandfather was not one to forget a promise. Shortly after his arrival on American soil, he established a fund for this specif-ic charity, naming it "Ezras Tzaddikim" – help for the righteous. The frequent collections he made in shuls were always preceded by his famous, generous pledge.

"I will match all the funds raised from this appeal," he would proclaim magnanimously.

Then, with a touch of humor, he would add, "Have no pity on me! Give as much as you can."

R' Hersh Meilich's generosity extended to various other areas as well. His house in Brownsville, New York seemed to possess revolving doors. Guests were constantly walking in and out of the Hecht home, adding much spice, laughter and hard work for the willing family members. My grandparents' stringent adherence to every nuance of religious observance was a well-known fact which magnetically attracted all visiting Rebbes from Europe and the Holy Land, as well as all religious Jews passing through Brownsville.

Yitta Draizel, R' Hersh Meilich's supportive and devoted wife, used to awaken at 2:00 A.M. Friday mornings to begin her feverish Shabbos preparations. The multitude of guests precipitated a multitude of baking and cooking which sometimes carried the dedicated woman on a cloud of activity until minutes before candle-lighting time. The absence of technological conveniences made it impossible to prepare any dishes in advance. An icebox was a solution to the problem, yet the Hechts usually stored their food outside during the frigid wintry months to prevent spoilage.

Kosher bakeries, groceries and meat markets were fantasies at that time, to be pondered wistfully in a rare moment of leisure. My grandmother cooked everything from scratch, from simple, basic dishes to delectable delicacies. The routine preparations involved in cooking chickens entailed a complicated procedure of countless hours. Bubby had to accompany the live chicken through all stages of its kosher slaughtering, soaking and salting before it was ready to be cooked for a meal.

R' Hersh Meilich's financial success as a well-to-do businessman and clothes manufacturer enabled the Hechts to host their guests comfortably. A minimum of ten guests were present at each Shabbos meal and the numbers often jumped to twenty-five or more. All and sundry were welcomed with open arms, and they departed with considerable donations for the organizations or Rabbinical courts they represented. Fundraisers would remain in the warm, hospitable home for weeks, appreciating the oasis of true Judaism in a country devoid of both – truth and Judaism.

Establishing Roots

The numerous guests seated at the Hecht's Shabbos table marveled at Zeide's generosity and unmitigated love for his Jewish brethren. They were but a small percentage of those privileged to receive a portion of his warmth and care. On a communal level, R' Hersh Meilich's altruistic efforts spanned large distances and a notable expanse of time.

"Rayim Ahuvim", the world-famous shtibel at Prospect Place, traces its roots back to an idealistic, energetic man in the early 1900's. Rabbi Hecht's unstinting efforts bore fruit in the form of a modest, two-family house which was converted to this prayer hall of infinite significance. The shtibel served as the home for many life-sustaining functions, acting as the all-encompassing heart of the Jewish community.

Minyonim were formed regularly on a daily basis, starting from the early morning hours and stretching until late evening. Most memorable of all were the gatherings on Shabbos and Yom Tov. Approximately one hundred men and teenagers congregated at the shtibel every Friday night, after finishing their meal at home. Upon their arrival at Rayim Ahuvim, they were welcomed by a warm, congenial atmosphere and ample refreshments. The cookies and cake, lima beans and chick peas, hot tea and cold beverages all faded into insignificance as the program commenced. Various classes were conducted by learned Rabbis to offer the hard-working individuals a taste of the wellsprings of Torah. Learned laymen formed private study groups and delved into the bottomless depths of Talmud, Midrash and Tanach. Two to three hours were spent in this manner, with the participants blissfully unaware of the steady passage of time. The cold reality of poverty and need was temporarily suffused with the warmth of the age-old Torah riches.

The poverty of the Brownsville residents was the cause of negligence in some vital aspects of their Jewish lifestyle. Some important traditions were unintentionally pushed into the abyss of oblivion by the ruthless hands of daily existence. Ritual immersion in a Mikveh was one of reality's uncalled for sacrifices. In an existence where a few pennies were the only boundary between slight hunger and starvation, the added expense of the Mikveh entrance fee was a luxury which most of them could not afford.

My saintly grandfather was appalled by this unacceptable, albeit unwilling, callousness to one of the fundamental aspects of Chassidus. Noted as one who suited thought to action, Zeide Hecht took upon himself the task of its immediate resurrection. Thus, he purchased a two-family house and transformed the simple duplex to a kosher Mikveh. All halachic requirements were stringently adhered to throughout its construction. The charge for use was minimal and it was therefore patronized by many. Its upkeep and maintenance were sponsored completely by R' Hersh Meilich, who accepted the expense as a privilege.

This Mikveh was renowned in Brownsville for its precise fulfillment of Halacha, and the Chassidic community held it in high regard. Therefore, when R' Yosef Yitzchok Schneersohn, the previous Lubavitcher Rebbe zal, requested directions to a reliable Mikveh, it came as no surprise that he was directed to Zeide's Mikveh.

In the year 1929, R' Yosef Yitzchok Schneersohn traveled across the world to awaken and inspire his Jewish brothers. The distant country, America, was especially in need of this fiery reminder, for proper Torah observance had become the badge of individuals rather than of communities. The Rebbe visited Chicago, Illinois and called for an immediate return to the nearly abandoned Mitzvos of Shabbos observance, Kashrus, and Jewish education. He forcefully proclaimed a message which echoed across the land of liberty.

"America is no different from Europe. The Torah way of life was good for our ancestors in Spain, Poland, Russia, France, Germany and England for close to one thousand years. It is most assuredly appropriate for America, too."

Rabbi Schneersohn personally carried this message to the largest synagogues in New York. Brownsville, being a notable center of Jewish residence, merited a visit of the holy personage. He arrived there on a Thursday afternoon and, first and foremost, requested the services of a proper Mikveh in honor of Shabbos.

When the request was forwarded to Zeide Hecht, he was catapulted into a storm of frenzied activity. Well-aware of the royalty and piety of the European Chassidic Rebbes, my grandfather insisted on perfecting the entire operation without any assistance. That fateful Friday found the Mikveh closed to the public. Only the venerable R' Hersh Meilich was to be found inside, assiduously scrubbing every crevice of the building, despite his advanced age. Fresh wooden planks were placed over the floor and new towels and mats were precisely laid out. Unsure of the Rebbe's preferences, my Zeide prepared a warm Mikveh as well as a cool one to suit his needs.

Taking note of the preparations made prior to his visit, the Rebbe extended a ten-dollar bill to my grandfather as a token of his sincere appreciation. Ten dollars was a princely sum in those times, but Zeide categorically refused the generous offer. The Ezras Tzaddikim had trained him to extend financial assistance to the Chassidic Rebbes of Europe. How could he possibly take money from them?

"Well, if that is your desire, allow me to grant you a blessing," the Rebbe responded.

"I bless you that your grandchildren will one day be my ardent Chassidim."

Zeide Hecht answered with a heartfelt "Amen". In the world of assimilation which characterized the American society at that time, it was difficult to imagine that one's descendants would steadfastly cling to their ancestors' ways. A blessing for Chassidic, religious offspring was as invaluable as it was unusual. Many years later, the treasured words took root in the hearts and minds of the young generation, bearing beautiful and everlasting fruits.

One would think that a man so instrumental in funding and sponsoring honorable causes and institutions would become accustomed to receiving honor and appreciation. R' Hersh Meilich Hecht proved otherwise. At an advanced age, Zeide decided to make a trip to Eretz Yisroel to visit Yeshivas Chayei Olam, which he served as the American gabbai for forty years. When the directors of the Yeshiva heard about the planned visit, they proceeded to prepare lavishly in honor of the esteemed guest who so generously funded the institution.

At the designated time, all prominent dignitaries awaited Rabbi Hecht's arrival at the portals of the Yeshiva. Long minutes of impatient waiting stretched into hours, and the much-anticipated visitor had yet to appear.

Unbeknownst to the erstwhile coordinators of the welcoming committee, my grandfather had surreptitiously slipped in through the back entrance. An unassuming figure clad in Chassidic garb, he seated himself in one of the dim corners of the large study hall and blissfully lost himself in the harmonious music of the Torah melodies. While the Yeshiva dignitaries tried to figure out the whereabouts of their esteemed donor, Mr. Hecht conducted his visit in the modest manner which he desired. His exit was as unpretentious as his entrance had been, and none were the wiser.

As Zeide Hecht made his final exit from this world, all those who wished to accord honor and respect to this beloved personage during his lifetime, streamed to do so upon his passing. His tragic death was connected to the projects and deeds which he had accomplished for the good of his brothers. A non-Jewish worker spotted R' Hersh Meilich standing near the vault which contained all the funds he had collected for charity. With uncontrolled greediness and ruthlessness, the worker tried to wrangle the considerable fortune out of the elderly man's grasp. In the ensuing struggle, a pure, unblemished soul was returned to its Maker, after more than eighty years of an utterly selfless existence.

R' Hersh Meilich Hecht's funeral in 1938 was one of the largest funerals ever seen in Brownsville. Thousands of Jews, who felt themselves orphaned upon his passing, came from all over the New York region to accompany him on his last journey. Although they felt their loss keenly, they found solace in the knowledge that his spirit would live on in the survival and continuity of American Jewry.

My Father's Home

R' Hersh Meilich's pious, generous spirit lived on in the noble actions and devout lifestyle of my father, R' Shia Hecht. Born in 1896 while my grandparents still resided on Manhattan's Lower East Side, little Shia was an active participant in the Hecht's renowned hospitality. My father's earliest memories all invariably included warmth, good cheer, and visiting European dignitaries.

At the turn of the twentieth century, there were barely any established institutions servicing the Orthodox communities. Recent immigrants were occupied with acclimating to their unfamiliar surroundings and making ends meet. Good yeshivos for their American-born sons were non-existent at that time and funds were unavailable to introduce this necessity. In its stead, inexperienced melamdim were employed to lead the children through the intricacies of Torah studies. The boys barely got past the basic, elementary rudiments of Mishna and Gemara.

Shia Hecht was no exception. In 1908, my grandfather spotted his twelve-year-old son and a friend carelessly playing with matches. The learned R' Hersh Meilich was appalled at the sight. How could Shia be occupied with such foolishness less than a year before to his Bar Mitzvah? In a couple of months he would be considered an adult, yet his childish actions seemed to prove otherwise. The gilded New World had deprived my father of the proper education that had been an accepted part of life in the European communities.

Disappointed and distressed, Zeide and Bubby Hecht reached a difficult, albeit unequivocal, decision. Their young son would have to cross the ocean in order to receive a thorough Torah education. The vast ocean that had distanced them from all that was familiar two decades ago would now carry their American son back home. The arduous journey would last minimally two weeks but the importance of Shia's Torah studies overshadowed all concerns of physical comfort.

My father studied in Yeshivas Chayei Olam in Yerushalayim for six productive years. R' Hersh Meilich was well acquainted with this august institution since he was its willing representative as the American gabbai. Satisfied with its high standards and warm atmosphere, he confidently placed his young son between its protective walls.

Throughout Shia's extended stay in Eretz Yisroel, he boarded in Batei Ungarin, in the neighborhood of Meah Shearim. He frequently visited the Lelover Rebbe who displayed a special fondness towards this young American scholar. The letters Shia sent home to his parents were infrequent due to the agonizingly slow process of overseas mail. R' Hersh Meilich and Yitta Dreizel forfeited the pleasure of their son's presence in deference to the ultimate pleasure. Their unmitigated joy at Shia's great strides in learning more than compensated for the constant pangs of worry and longing.

The year 1914 marked the onset of World War I and my father's long-awaited homecoming. My grandparents were ecstatic as they welcomed home their eighteen-year-old son. Six years in Yeshiva had transformed the carefree young lad into a budding Talmud Chochom and R' Hersh Meilich was infinitely proud of his unbelievable achievements.

In Greenpoint, a Brooklyn neighborhood quite a distance from Brownsville, another family rejoiced upon hearing about

Shia Hecht's homecoming. R' Yehoshua Auster, or R' Shialeh, as he was affectionately called, made careful inquiries about the Hecht family in general and about Shia, in particular. The Auster household was delighted with the sparkling reports they received on the young man's uncompromising religious observance and his astounding breadth of Torah knowledge. R' Shialeh, a pious Galitzianer Chassid, had nearly despaired in his search for the fitting life partner for his daughter, Sorah. The gilded American cage had trapped majority of the Jewish youth in its glittery confines. Shia Hecht, the prospective groom, was one of the few hardy individuals who had managed to avoid the enticing clutches.

Meanwhile, in Brownsville, R' Hersh Meilich embarked on a search of his own as he tried to establish the future of his refined, learned 'son'. His questions produced remarkable results. The Auster family living on Sumner Avenue in Greenpoint, New York, was renowned and well-respected for their warmth and piety. R' Shialeh gave a shiur every Friday night and Shabbos morning in the local shul. During these well-attended classes, he delved into the commentary of R' Chaim Ben Attar, the "Ohr Hachaim".

One wintry Friday afternoon, two feet of snow were unceremoniously dumped on the New York streets. The blizzard was considered bothersome by most, but to one lone traveler it seemed absolutely disastrous. R' Shialeh was on the way home from work, and the trolley he was traveling in was placidly turtling its way through the unexpected snowdrifts. Neither the irate passengers nor the trolley car's jerky movements were responsible for the loss of his usual equanimity. It was the lengthening rays of the setting sun which planted in him some germinating seeds of panic. The Shabbos queen was literally standing at the world's doorstep, and one of her sons was still seated on a traveling vehicle.

R' Shialeh wasted no time in solving this unprecedented problem. Walking over to the frustrated conductor, he calmly handed over his wallet, which contained most of his weekly earnings.

"The onset of our Shabbos is imminent and since we may not carry our belongings then, I was hoping you would hold this for me until tomorrow evening," R' Shialeh explained hurriedly.

Disregarding the curious glances being thrown his way, he stepped off the trolley car and started walking home. The bitter cold was piercing but his soul was aflame with pure devotion. It was this fiery warmth that melted all worries about the uncertain fate of his fortune.

After the departure of that memorable Shabbos, a respectful knock on the door announced the presence of the trolley-car conductor. He stood at the entrance of the Auster residence and wordlessly handed over R' Shialeh's sacrifice. The wallet and its valuable contents were returned, completely intact. Shabbos had obviously spread its protection over this loyal Jew.

R' Shialeh was, apparently, uncompromising in every detail which characterized the lifestyle of a religious Jew. Consequently, his daughter was brought up in a home full of joy and Torah harmoniously intertwined. Zeide Hecht was more than satisfied and Zeide Auster felt the same way. Within a short while, my parents, R' Shia and Sorah Hecht, were married in a modest, strictly religious ceremony. After all necessary preliminaries had been arranged, a truly Yiddishe home in every sense of the word, was firmly established. The American soil resisted their efforts at every turn, but their roots were only strengthened by the adverse conditions.

The strong roots soon sprouted into a beautiful tree boasting six fresh, young branches. My five brothers and I were born in a span of ten years and we colored life in the Hecht home with exuberant, spirited strokes. Shlomo Zalman was born in 1918, Moshe Yitzchok in 1920, and I followed in 1922. Two years later, Yaakov made his appearance followed by Peretz in 1926 and Sholom in 1928.

Blessed with a young, growing family, my father was hard-pressed to meet the daily demands. At first he was employed as a salesman, but later on he opened his own wholesale dry goods store. The sole proprietorship was a lucrative business and financial concerns were therefore non-existent. My childhood memories bring to mind neither extravagant expenditures nor undue scrimping. Life then was simply an adventure-filled ocean flowing smoothly along the heimishe Brownsville streets.

A Carefree Childhood

My brothers and I made sure that there was never a dull moment in the Hecht home. Our boisterous spirits and unquenchable enthusiasm infused each passing day with life and action. Despite the growing demands of his young family, my father firmly established the kindness and charity he had witnessed as a child, in his own home. Rabbis and respected dignitaries from Europe and Eretz Yisroel were always welcomed into our home for a refreshing meal or an extended stay.

Our excitement at the arrival of guests made us immune to the hardships involved in sleeping on the dining room floor. My parents gave up their bedroom for distinguished visitors, and when more than one guest stayed at our home we willingly relinquished our beds.

I remember how my father used to insist on giving up his own seat at the head of the table, in deference to a rabbinical guest. Thus, the Rabbi would be honored with leading our Shabbos meals as if he actually presided over the entire household. Mama respectfully served the sumptuous dishes she had worked long and hard to prepare. What really made an indelible impression on me, as a youngster, was my father's ritual when preparing the guests' sleeping quarters. Although my brothers and I were capable of arranging all necessary details, Tatte refused to relinquish the coveted privilege. He personally provided fresh linen and blankets for each visitor, as well as negel vasser and a towel for when they woke up. These significant deeds were never considered a burden, for Tatte felt honored to service his righteous guests.

The details of one visit in particular remain engraved in my memory due to the unprecedented incident it sparked off. The Riglitzer Rebbe had arrived from Europe and we joyfully welcomed him into our home. Friday night, the dignified Rebbe accompanied us to the Sefardishe Kloiz for the Shabbos prayers.

The Sefardishe Kloiz was the shul that my father had established in Brownsville. Tatte's shul, along with the Rayim Ahuvim shtibel that Zeide Hecht had founded, the Polisher shtibel, and the shul of Yeshivas Chaim Berlin, were the only four synagogues servicing the Brownsville community. The elected officials presiding on the shul committees tried to maintain the homey atmosphere that the immigrants remembered from Europe. Many old-timers frequented the flourishing shuls and their memorable personalities left a profound impression on me as a young child.

I recall Rabbi Esrog's passionate prayers, accompanied with tears of deep emotion. This elderly man from Eretz Yisroel prayed with extreme devotion that seemed to envelop him in elevated flames of fire. R' Shialeh Belzer, a member of Zeide Hecht's shtibel, was always greatly disturbed when a non-Jewish language was used in shul.

"Sheigatz, arois fun shul!"

Whenever I heard this enraged scolding I knew that the scholarly elder had heard some unfortunate young man speaking English between the four holy walls of Rayim Ahuvim. His vehement protests certainly diminished the amount of English spoken in his vicinity, for no one wanted to be subjected to R' Shialeh Belzer's proverbial tongue-lashing.

The Sefardishe Kloiz also had its share of personalities, dignitaries and scholars. Rabbi Ziskin the shamash, for example, came to the conclusion that the laws of prohibition were irrelevant to the members of the shul. The Chassidim were accustomed to drinking the fiery liquid at festive occasions and the loyal sha-mash thought it quite improper of the government to deprive them of this particular tradition. Therefore, he kept his own se-cret distillery in the shul's basement where the illegal beverages were produced at an alarming rate.

Generally, warmth and congeniality characterized our shul's existence but sometimes the overworked members expressed their distress in a manner which angered my father. The Riglitzer Rebbe's visit was an occasion that ignited Tatte's fury to a de-gree I had never previously witnessed.

After the Shabbos morning prayers, the Riglitzer Rebbe start-ed making his way towards the podium to deliver a speech. The president of the shul was exhausted from the long week and couldn't control his impatience. Walking over to the Rebbe, he brusquely informed him, "You're not going to speak here today!"

My father heard the crude remark and his eyes sparked with fury. How could someone display such blatant disrespect toward a renowned Torah scholar? With measured steps, Tatte ap-proached the president of the shul and delivered a resounding slap. Quiet prevailed in the Sefardishe Kloiz as the Riglitzer Rebbe gave over a fiery sermon. Tatte's action might have seemed extreme, but it was simply an expression of the deep re-spect he harbored for the Torah and its representatives.

This was the chinuch we received at home as well as in our grandparents' homes. Zeide and Bubby Hecht resided in Browns-ville and my brothers and I greatly enjoyed their proximity. Zeide and Bubby Auster in Greenpoint lived quite a distance from us but we frequently went to visit the little house on Sum-ner Avenue. The Shabbosim we spent there as young children were filled with warmth, serenity and enthralling stories. My grandfather couldn't afford to leave the electricity on all Shabbos so tall, majestic candles were used instead. During the Friday night seudah, the dining room was bathed in the soft, hazy glow of the Shabbos flames. Although we were an energetic, lively bunch, the magical atmosphere kept us glued to our seats as Zeide told miracle stories of the Baal Shem Tov and other Chassidic Rebbes. Our young minds were captivated by the miraculous events of bygone eras and the inherent joy of Chassidus.

Once on a regular weekday, while I was visiting my grandparents in Greenpoint, I was awakened in the middle of the night by the sounds of heart-wrenching sobs. Baffled and more than a little frightened, I crept out of bed and pulled open the creaking bedroom door. The full moon cast a pale, silvery glow along the darkened corridor. I cautiously headed toward the kitchen and stood at the doorway in fear. Sitting on the floor with tears streaming down his face, Zeide suddenly appeared so old and forlorn. His broken cries tore at my heart and my imagination immediately conjured up the possible causes of this distressing sight.

Soft footsteps behind me quietly announced Bubby's arrival. She gently took me by the hand and led me back to bed.

"Bubby," I started breathlessly, "why is Zeide crying?"

Bubby looked at me intently in the dimly lit room and explained, "He's reciting tikkun chatzos, a prayer which mourns the destruction of the Bais Hamikdosh."

I stared at my grandmother in wide-eyed wonder, trying to fathom Zeide's obvious pain. At that time, I was too young to fully understand his piety and the depth of his yearning for the redemption, but those heartfelt tears left an indelible impression on my young mind. Until today, I am unaware of how frequently my saintly grandfather mourned the Temple's destruction, but Bubby was apparently accustomed to this midnight scene.

After Bubby Auster passed away in 1928, Zeide remarried and emigrated to Eretz Yisroel. Thus, when my oldest brother, Shlomo Zalman, crossed the Atlantic at the age of twelve to study in a good yeshiva, he took up residence with our beloved grandfather. In 1935, seven years after he had left home, Shlomo Zalman returned as a mature, learned young man and he continued his studies in Yeshivas Torah V'daas in Williamsburg. The rest us were enrolled there too as soon as we reached high-school age. Traveling daily was a small price to pay for the thorough Jewish education we received in the flourishing land of liberty. After all, my father had to travel halfway across the world to merit the schooling we took for granted. In comparison to Tatte's sacrifice, Yeshivas Torah V'daas was located in our own backyard.

29

Yeshiva Tales

Before I began my schooling in Torah V'daas in Williamsburg, I learned in Yeshivas Chaim Berlin. The yeshiva was situated only half a block from my home in Brownsville, but that was its only advantage. My schooling began a year later than was usual, for I started only in the second grade. I had heard uncomplimentary reports on the first-grade teacher, and, being quite a headstrong young lad, I adamantly refused to place myself under his tutelage. To my surprise, my illogical complaints had the desired effect and I gained another year of unrestricted freedom. My subsequent experiences in yeshiva convinced me of the validity of my childish opposal to school attendance.

In the late 1920's, the yeshiva was poorly run due to a deficiency of English-speaking Orthodox Jews. Yeshivas Chaim Berlin was founded by immigrants concerned with the continuation and establishment of the way of life that had been part and parcel of every European community. Unfortunately, these immigrants knew only a smattering of English and they therefore had to employ educated American Jews to run their yeshiva. Modern and educated, these appointed officials were not particularly worried about the necessity of every nuance inherent in proper Jewish observance. Thus, many of my teachers were known to be maskilim who cynically disposed of the numerous, treasured traditions that we held so dear. I distinctly recall my initial feelings of horror when I heard that someone had spotted one of my esteemed teachers proudly boarding the trolley on a sunny Shabbos afternoon. How could this revered personage who professed to be teaching me the secrets of life so brazenly transgress the holy day of rest? Understandably, my respect for this particular teacher became a thing of the past as I contemplated the implications of his inappropriate conduct.

This teacher was not an exception. Most of the staff members employed at that time made sure to give over their subject matter in the spirit of the haskalah, thus imperceptibly implanting potential danger in our young minds. Others were inexperienced immigrants who had absolutely no understanding of the needs of American youth. Their lessons were labeled uninspiring at best and unbearably boring when we were not so charitable. As a result, the level of education was pathetically low and did nothing for our attachment to Judaism. Despite the desperate need to keep us youngsters interested and enthusiastic about the religion so often looked down upon, our elementary-school years did quite the opposite.

Rabbi Besdansky and Rabbi Pam, the father of Rav Avraham Pam zt"l, were two notable exceptions to the unfortunate reality. They taught the seventh and eighth grades respectively, and their superb teaching skills erased much of the erroneous education we had been subjected to in earlier years. Both of them hailed from Lithuania and, unlike many others, they carefully preserved the essence and enjoyment of Torah life throughout the long journey across the ocean. The lure of liberty and freedom proved to be a weak contestant to their staunch, unshakable belief in Hashem. Aside from the truth and purity we glimpsed in their noble ways, they were outstanding rebbeim who knew how to ignite the love of Torah and Yiddishkeit in each of their students.

Rabbi Besdansky and Rabbi Pam considerably sweetened my memories of the years spent in Yeshivas Chaim Berlin but I was more than glad to join Shlomo Zalman and Moshe Yitzchok in Torah V'daas when I graduated eighth grade. The serious, untainted atmosphere was conducive to our Torah studies and I reveled in the absence of corruptive influences. My two brothers, already deeply involved in every aspect of yeshiva life, greatly eased my adjustment to the unfamiliar sense of rigidity and uniformity that characterized Yeshivas Torah V'daas on Bedford Avenue and Taylor Street. Shlomo Zalman, the oldest of the Hecht clan, had become well-acquainted with one of his fellow students, Avrohom Barnetsky. This relationship was the catalyst of many significant changes that swept up our entire family on the fervent wings of Chassidus.

Avrohom had been attending weekly study groups formed by an energetic man whose indomitable personality and warmth attracted members of all ages and stages. Rabbi Yisroel Jacobson had reached the American shores in 1925 with the encouragement of the previous Lubavitcer Rebbe, R' Yosef Yitzchok Schneersohn. As his parents and siblings had done a few years before him, Rabbi Jacobson settled in New York and proceeded to make his mark in the incurable rush of city life. Within a short time of his arrival in Brownsville, he had assumed the position of Rabbi in a small shul which included members of his distant hometown, Zhurovitch, located in White Russia. Fueled by the blessings of the Lubavitcher Rebbe and seeking to plant some seeds of inspiration in America's barren soil, Rabbi Jacobson became involved in the enrichment and nourishment of Brownsville's community life.

Rabbi Jacobson's weekly gatherings were associated with warmth, congeniality and an awe-inspiring depth of Torah study. At times, he would regal the devoted members with fascinating tales of Chassidic Rebbes and noteworthy personalities in the annals of Jewish history. Relaxed by the informal stance of this learned individual, the teenagers and young men would share their thoughts, questions and quandaries with one whom they knew could be trusted. With an unusual amount of patience and understanding, Rabbi Jacobson resolved their problems and cleared up their confusion.

It came as no surprise, therefore, when Shlomo Zalman was enthralled after his first introduction to these voluntary classes. Avrohom Barnetsky had given my brother a small taste of what constituted true Chassidus and before long we all became weekly visitors in the Jacobson home. Zeide Hecht zt"l had received a blessing from the Lubavitcher Rebbe that his offspring would become devout Lubavitcher Chassidim and these weekly farbrengen were the first indications of its realization.

In the spring of 1938, our house resounded with the sounds and feelings accompanying every Jewish simcha. My brother, Shlomo Zalman, had gotten engaged to Chaya Sarah, the oldest daughter of our esteemed mentor and guide. My father and Rabbi Yisroel Jacobson found themselves in great company as they worked together on the preparations for this joyous event. Getting ready for a wedding is no simple matter, as we were soon priviliged to understand. While Mama feverishly took care of many materialistic details, Shlomo Zalman proceeded to arrange his spiritual matters. At the time of his betrothal, my brother had firmly decided to grow a beard and the constant gossip of neighbors and friends didn't deter him in the least. A sight which had been so common in most of the European communities was considered peculiar in the new, modernized world of America. Passerby would sadly shake their heads, murmuring with marked sympathy that the "Hecht's oldest son had obviously gone out of his mind".

Shlomo Zalman simply shrugged his shoulders and proceeded to embark on his personal campaign. His bold decision was emulated by a number of fellow students who understood the truth and pride which accompany such an important step. Curious stares and spiteful jeering were no match for the steadfast determination of these courageous young men. If a beard was considered appropriate for the Jews in Europe, it was most definitely appropriate for those distanced from the communities of old by an arduous journey and a paltry few years.

This unexpected decision paled in comparison to the bombshell which Shlomo Zalman dropped unceremoniously soon after the wedding festivities had ended. We were shocked by the sheer absurdity of the young couple's plans for their future, but careful introspection revealed that they were not as unrealistic as previously conceived. My oldest brother had decided to once again cross the ocean and establish his home on the other side. Yeshivas Tomchei Temimim was pulling him strongly from afar and his young wife eagerly offered her unshakable support. They planned to settle down in Otwock, a small suburb on the outskirts of Warsaw, where both the Lubavitcher Rebbe and the yeshiva he had established were located.

Possessing a strong will and a strong conviction of the importance of this journey, Shlomo Zalman convinced two of his friends to follow suit. Avrohom Barnetsky and Dov Ber Levy enthusiastically conferred with my brother on the details, advantages and disadvantages of taking such a drastic step. Barely two months after we celebrated the wedding of our oldest brother, we escorted him and his young wife to the plank of the vessel which would spirit them away in search of spiritual growth and fulfillment.

My dear parents experienced strong feelings of deja vu as they once again parted from their firstborn. When he was a young lad of twelve years, they had convinced him of the importance of traversing such large distances in order to merit a solid Torah education. Now, as a grown man of twenty years, Shlomo Zalman had convinced his parents of the sacrifices necessary to establish a home based on Torah and Chassidus in the proper surroundings. Their acceptance was accompanied by a surge of pride at the proof that the concepts they had tried to instill in their children had obviously taken root.

We're Off!

The year 1939 is a year that is etched in blood and tears. Its numbers are doomed to carry a heavy burden of guilt, helplessness and loss for all generations. The passage of time has muted the cries of agony and separation but the heartbreaking echoes will never be quieted. Jews living in Europe at that ominous time held their breaths in fear as they anxiously followed the horrific developments. Their American brethren did likewise as they tried to grasp concepts that were beyond human explanation. Those lucky enough to procure the required documents were allowed to abandon the burning European shores and start a new life in a friendlier land.

In August of that fateful year, six American boys chose to do just the opposite. They were well-aware of the danger involved in crossing the ocean at such ominous times, but the fire in their souls easily consumed the fire of war. Despite the instability that was sweeping across the European continent, the seventeen- to twenty-year-old boys were determined to merit learning in Otwock, under the great Lubavitcher Rebbe of whom they had heard so much. Their parents were, understandably, adamant in their refusal to this ill-timed venture, and the idealistic teenagers were forced to agree.

One of the boys, Mordechai Fisher, sent a letter to the Rebbe explaining that their trip was cancelled due to their parents' well-founded hesitation. The reply he received set the wheels in motion oncc again.

"You have nothing to fear," the Rebbe had written, and for his young chassidim that was more than enough.

When I heard about this unexpected reply, my heart soared at the door of opportunity that had suddenly opened up for our small, Europe-bound group. Rabbi Yisroel Jacobson, our mentor who had first introduced us to the world of chassidus, wasted no time in making the necessary arrangements. The date of the planned journey was set for Friday, August 4, and there was still an inordinate amount of details to take care of before that long-awaited day arrived.

Overwhelmed with excitement, I informed my parents of our plans, hoping for a grudging approval. Their response was an un-equivocal "no" due to the danger involved in taking up residence in the European powder-keg. Shlomo Zalman and his young wife, Chaya Sarah, were still situated in that distant continent and my parents were sick with worry over their uncertain future. Sending another son into the battlefield was a sacrifice they were not willing to make.

I understood their misgivings but I couldn't accept their deci-sion as final. Passport applications cost fifteen dollars, an exorbi-tant fee at that time. My father would certainly refuse to sponsor what he termed a hare-brained adventure, so I withdrew the re-quired funds from my own bank account that had been set up with my bar-mitzvah gifts. Accompanied by Rabbi Jacobson, I vis-ited the passport office and painstakingly filled out a pile of forms. It would take quite a while for my passport to arrive in the post and I fervently prayed that I would get it before the date of departure. Our voyage had been postponed to Wednes-day, the ninth of August, but as the weeks followed each other with unprecedented languidity, my passport had still not arrived.

Monday morning, a mere two days before our planned depar-ture, I watched dawn break over the dark New York streets. Beset with worry, I impulsively ran out of the house at 6:00 A.M. and headed toward the local post office. The deserted streets attested to the unearthly hour, but anxiety had eradicated every trace of logical reasoning and behavior. The post office was understandably still locked and I proceeded to knock urgently on the closed door. The loud banging resounded like drum rolls in my ears, encouraging me to continue with my relentless efforts. From time to time, I placed my ear close to the wooden door, but only a mocking silence emanated from within.

"What are you doing here, boy?" an irate night worker yelled, after unlocking the heavily bolted door.

"Don't you know that it ain't morning yet? Why, your knocking is loud enough to wake the dead!"

Relieved that my incessant attempts had produced results, I speedily explained the purpose of my early visit. The guard softened somewhat when he realized that without a passport I would be unable to travel with my companions to Europe on Wednesday.

"Oh, alright, young lad. I'll go check if anything came for you today. Just do me a favor – don't make these early-morning visits a regular habit, okay?"

Once again, I faced the closed wooden door and fervently prayed for deliverance. After a few interminable moments, the beaming security guard wordlessly handed over the precious document. The long-awaited passport stared up at me gleefully, as if urging me to explore the spiritual paradise on the other side of the vast ocean. After profusely thanking the guard, I started heading home on the exuberant wings of hope.

The early hour notwithstanding, I enthusiastically bounded up the stairs and into the kitchen. The good news was begging to be told and refused to be subjected to the dictates of reason.

"Mama, look what I have!" I exclaimed, proudly waving my passport in the air.

Mama was shocked at the news and quickly woke up Tatte to

hear his opinion. My parents had been unaware of the fact that I had even applied for a passport. My initiative proved to them how important this perilous journey was to their young son and they therefore grudgingly gave their approval. It was just two days before our journey was due to begin, so Mama was immediately catapulted into a frenzy of preparation. Gathering the belongings to ease my adjustment in the distant land was her method of dealing with the burden of worry and apprehension.

Tatte accompanied me to various embassies in order to procure the necessary visas. A new set of clothing was purchased in honor of the journey and each acquisition seemed to crystallize the unbelievable reality. I was going to join my brother who was situated somewhere on the other side of the globe, and Tatte had even given me his blessing. The gathering clouds of a threatening, stormy war were unable to obstruct my view of life's beautiful sunlight. When a dream materializes, all other concerns fade into oblivion despite their actual significance.

Two days of absolute chaos and pandemonium struck our little house, pulling all inhabitants along on a turbulent ride. Wednesday morning dawned bright and clear, in conjunction to my infectious, upbeat attitude. Accompanied by my concerned parents, I traveled to the New York harbor where I met Rabbi Jacobson and my five fellow students. Mordechai Dov Altein, Meir Greenberg, Zorach Gordon, Yitzchok Kolodny and Mordechai Fisher had excitement written across their faces whereas our group coordinator, Rabbi Jacobson, seemed anxious to begin the long, arduous journey. Word of our planned trip abroad had slipped into the homes of all the Lubavitcher Chassidim in New York, and their response was overwhelming. Most of them had made the effort to see us off at the harbor, and they joined our parents and families in wordless prayer and boundless hope. Spirits were high that summer morning as was evidenced by the exuberant dancing and singing spontaneously conducted prior to our ship's departure. The officials standing stiffly at their posts had never witnessed such a lively gathering of Chassidic Jews and they obviously enjoyed the sight. The "Isle de France", as our ship was pompously called, was scheduled to leave at precisely 11:30 A.M., without any excess consideration for our unexpected assemblage. American Orthodox Jews watched with unconcealed yearning as seven of their own boarded the vessel headed to a land soaked in spirituality. Without being told, we knew intuitively that we had been charged with the heavy responsibility of acting as the representatives of New York's growing communities.

Rabbi Jacobson enthusiastically led the way and his six young charges confidently followed. Our worried mothers uttered last-minute instructions that were heard only by the indifferent seagulls, while our fathers followed our departing figures with meaningful glances of hope, anxiety and encouragement. I waved to the disappearing figures standing so forlornly on shore as their young sons seemed to disappear behind the horizon. Who knows what awaited them in that distant area. Would they be arriving to a glorious display of spiritual color, only to encounter disappointment when they realized that it was the hues of a sun setting on a vibrant world of Torah? Would the red-hot flames of war obstruct the path of undisturbed Torah study? Would these very same flames conquer the warmth of Chassidus that so strongly pulled their sons' searching souls?

Oblivious to our parents' well-founded worries, our little group immensely enjoyed the first few days of the journey. The invigorating ocean air, combined with a strong sense of purpose and unity, kept our spirits on an elevated plateau where war and strife were unable to infringe. The kosher food we had brought along kept us satisfied physically, while the wisdom of our revered leader took care of our spiritual needs. I remember sitting on the deck late one night and singing together harmoniously. The Chassidic melodies infused me with a complete happiness that I had never previously conceived possible. After the last strains of our spontaneous burst of song had faded into the murky depths of our watery surroundings, I was overcome with a strong feeling of pride at the obvious truth and fulfillment that characterizes the existence of a religious Jew.

Three days after we had boarded the ship, we all became violently seasick, thus bringing an abrupt end to the pleasurable hours spent on deck. Fortunately, it wasn't too long before we caught our first glimpse of the European continent. We reached the coast of Cornwall, England just as the sun was majestically rising over the placid waters. The awe-inspiring view, coupled with the undisturbed serenity of the shore at dawn, seemed to be promising us an uplifting experience in this land which our parents still thought of as home.

41

Arrival at Otwock, 1939

Our journey on water continued until late Monday evening, when we arrived at the French port of Le Havre. Delighted with the feeling of firm ground under our feet, we soon had to find our seats on a moving vehicle once again. A train delivered us to the bustling capital city of Paris, where we were met by Rabbi Schneur Zalman Schneersohn, a prominent Lubavitcher Chassid. Weary from the seemingly endless wandering, our exhausted group greatly enjoyed the short respite in his home where we ate our first warm meal since our departure from the American shores. As soon as supper was consumed, we headed towards the train terminal in order to begin the last leg of our extended journey.

To our extreme pleasure and surprise, we met Rabbi Mendel Schneersohn, the Rebbe's second son-in-law, at the terminal. He had been sent to greet us before the long train ride to Warsaw, Poland. At first glance, I sized him up as a young man in his thirties, with a nice beard, and a gray hat. Upon further inspection, I noted the piety and purity streaming forth from his friendly, welcoming countenance and the exalted level of kedusha he had reached at such a young age. We felt privileged to be in his company before the train carried us past towns and cities in various countries.

The Rebbe's son-in-law stood on the steps of the train as he patiently and warmly greeted us. He told us of the great zechus we had to go to Otwock to be in the presence of the Rebbe and to become his students. He blessed us and wished us succes in our studies.

Sleep was understandably quite a luxury in such conditions, for the train's hard benches weren't exactly the epitome of comfort. The constant jolting and occasional stops kept us awake throughout the last part of our journey. At 5:00 A.M., we fervently began the Shacharis prayers as the Belgian scenery flashed by the grimy windows. The thought of what lay ahead of us infused our daily prayers with an unprecedented devotion and renewal and completely eradicated any bothersome signs of sleep deprivation. It wasn't until 9:30 in the evening that we arrived at the Polish border.

"Platzen sie, aber sitzen sie," the Polish officer repeated insistently in German, asking everyone to remain seated calmly until the routine document checks were completed.

Rabbi Jacobson reassured us that there was nothing to fear, since legally we were all well within our rights. Despite this comforting piece of information, I felt my heartbeat speeding up as the officer approached our impatient group. No one enjoys being put under inspection, especially at a time when avid hostility is directed specifically at one's nation.

"What is the purpose of this trip?" the officer inquired formally.

When he heard our innocent reply that we had come to Europe in order to progress in our studies, the boorish official could not contain his derision. War was obviously imminent, and he couldn't fathom why American Jews would risk their lives for such a purpose. He was certain that America offered more advanced courses and methods of study, which put the European techniques in an unobtrusive corner of shame.

"Schtudiren? Seinen sie verukt? (To study? Are you crazy?)" he proclaimed disdainfully.

Slightly miffed at his uncomplimentary statement, we simply

handed over our passports for inspection and hoped that we wouldn't be deported on some false pretext borne of his obvious hate and disgust. Our fears proved to be unfounded, for all the documents were grudgingly approved and returned.

After an interminable amount of time wasted on formalities and trivialities, our train was finally given the signal to cross the border and enter Poland. Having been forewarned about the notorious thievery prevalent in the Polish society, I kept my hand firmly in my pocket to ensure that my precious passport would not become the property of some gleeful vagabond. Judging from the dirty looks and intolerable attitude of our fellow travelers, I didn't think that I would receive any help or sympathy if someone tried to requisition it.

Thus, upon sighting the sign announcing our arrival to Warsaw, I breathed an audible sigh of relief and withdrew my hand from my pocket. Our final destination was now within our reach and our enthusiasm dispelled all thoughts of home, hunger, and danger. An entire ocean and several train rides separated us from our immediate families, causing us to willingly adopt the Lubavitcher Yeshiva as our second home even before we entered its protective embrace.

On Rosh Chodesh Elul, precisely a week after our ship had set sail from the New York harbor, we arrived in Otwock, a pleasant outer suburb of Warsaw. Yeshivas Tomchei Temimim, housed in a modest, non-descript building, magically restored our flagging strength and wordlessly called out a warm welcome to its foreign visitors. Undefined expectations hovered in the air as we proceeded to the entrance of the yeshiva, and a strange feeling of hesitation met us at the door.

As soon as we stepped over the threshold, our apprehension evaporated and our illogical fear scurried away in shame. The sight that met our eyes was as astonishing as it was invigorating. Approximately four hundred students were swaying over their seforim, alternating between vehement arguments and occasional concessions. The air was soaked with an intense concentration coupled with an unquenchable thirst for knowledge and true love of Torah. I blinked my eyes in disbelief, hoping that the mirage wouldn't disappear like an imaginary oasis in the desert. Oblivious to the fact that their actions were being observed by their American counterparts, the boys continued to delve into their studies and untangle the challenging complications.

I would have gladly remained at the sidelines drinking in the wondrous sounds and sight of Torah, but our little group was politely directed to the Rosh Yeshiva's office. After carefully weaving our way through the swaying sea of black and white, we were greeted by Rabbi Yehudah Eber, a brilliant Chassidic scholar who had escaped from the Soviet Union a few years previous. After arriving in Otwock, he had been appointed as the Rosh Yeshiva of Tomchei Temimim.

Rabbi Eber welcomed us warmly to Europe in general and to the Lubavitcher community of Otwock in particular. In a relaxed manner, he proceeded to test the depth and breadth of knowledge we possessed in Talmudic studies, as well as in the concepts and teachings of Chassidus. I was placed in Rabbi Eber's class, the yeshiva's highest Talmudic class, and my five companions were assigned to their classes as well. Infused with the inspiration abounding in the yeshiva's large study hall, I felt ready to learn for several hours without interruption.

The yeshiva administration had arranged lodgings for the "spoiled" American boys in the home of a widow who resided close to Yeshivas Tomchei Temimim. In contrast to the conditions that adequately served the needs of the Polish boys, we were provided with a more comfortable apartment in deference to the "luxurious" lifestyle we led in America. We still had difficulties adjusting to the so-called comforts, such as the sacks of straw that were unfittingly titled "beds". Accustomed as we were to mattresses and warm quilts, we had to alter our expectations to accommodate sacks of straw and flimsy excuses for blankets.

One night, the summer heat was simply unbearable. The humidity seemed to be rising drastically as we unsuccessfully tried to welcome sleep into our stifling room. Without any undue considerations, we opened all of our bedroom windows to allow some air to circulate. Our innocent action did more harm than good, for in Poland, an open window is a clear invitation to the thieves prowling the streets at night. To our extreme consternation, the rising sun threw light on our grievous error. Our passports, money and watches had all disappeared in the darkness of the previous night, leaving us bereft of our most valuable belongings.

The proceedings added a good deal of humor to our desperate situation. The Polish policemen arrived at our apartment, looking like caricatures of medieval detectives. Large magnifying glasses were pompously extracted from their voluminous pockets as they importantly went about their business. We tried to prevent our laughter from bubbling up as we wordlessly followed the comical proceedings. The police officers used their ridiculous magnifying glasses to find some non-existent fingerprints on all possible surfaces in our bedroom.

A short while later we admitted with a minimal amount of respect that the Polish police force was not as incompetent as we had assumed. Our passports were returned as well as a pair of pants that the thieves had deemed worthy of attention. Lingering suspicions about the methods the police employed to return our stolen property receded to insignificance as we became involved in the daily goings-on of yeshiva life.

Breakfast and supper was prepared for us by the kindly widow whom we boarded by, but at lunchtime we were left to our own devices. A small grocery was located a short distance from the yeshiva, but its unappetizing products made hunger a preferred option. The European students greatly appreciated the apples, moldy hard cheese and rotting vegetables for their midday meal, but we found it impossible to settle on such unsavory morsels.

Another factor that highlighted our American roots was the manner in which we spent the short breaks we had between classes. I recall the astounded reactions of our new friends as we pulled out bats, balls and mitts for an impromptu game of baseball. The sport was unfamiliar in Europe at that time, and the mere thought of running around in a heated game of baseball during yeshiva hours was unheard of. Our occasional boxing matches really aroused their wonder and curiosity. At first, the students had wondered why we had brought along such large gloves from home if we had arrived during the blazing heat of August. When the use of these gloves became apparent during the first boxing match, their wonder increased tenfold. After all, such an open display of supposed violence went against their ingrained principles of propriety and dignity.

Adjusting to our new environment was a challenge but we met it with the enthusiasm and vigor characteristic of youth. The illustrious Talmudei Chachomim and the astounding depth of Torah study we witnessed in our numerous classes fulfilled our hopes and dreams in a manner we had never thought possible.

46

Disrupted Haven

Two days after our arrival in Otwock, I felt that my life was suffused with an unprecedented degree of warmth and sunshine. The adjustment period we had been warned about was considerably easier than predicted and our acclimation process was nearly complete. Primitive living conditions and unsatisfying meals were minor inconveniences that soon became an accepted part of our new lifestyle. We marveled at the advanced level of serious learning and the atmosphere of togetherness generated by a community striving in unity toward the same goals.

On our first Friday afternoon in Poland, we were treated to an additional portion of illumination that placed our previous satisfaction in the shadows. The six American students were privileged to enter the Lubavitcher Rebbe's study for the first time, in order to hear a maamar, a discourse on Chassidic philosophy. Our anticipation skyrocketed as the clock finally struck the designated hour, and we followed Rabbi Jacobson into the room.

My impressions of the short half-hour we spent there have remained vividly engraved in my mind despite the considerable passage of time. Even now, many years older and wiser, I find it difficult to describe that memorable experience. The words spoken were hard to understand but the Rebbe's shining face, filled with love and holiness, required no explanations. I distinctly felt the presence of something far beyond limited human understanding and was awed by its obvious truth and purity. As I reluctantly exited the room after the short maamar, I knew with unparalleled certainty that this quiet town in Poland signified much more than a mere replacement for home.

Day followed day in beautific succession as my friends and I thirstily absorbed the essence of Torah study, Torah thoughts, and most importantly, a way of life based on these lofty teachings. America seemed more distant than the moon, and just as irrelevant. A full week passed with the speed of light as I immersed myself in the shiurim with vigor and invincible enthusiasm. When we were informed that we would once again be admitted into the Rebbe's study on our second Friday in Otwock, a full blown thunderstorm couldn't have obliterated the boundless sunshine.

"Teshuva tefillah u'tzedaka maavirin es ro'a hagzeirah."

The Rebbe began this discourse on an ominous note, due to the unsettling rumblings of war that were threatening our peaceful existence. I listened intently to the carefully measured words and to my surprise, I managed to understand their meaning. My euphoria at the sudden clarity was slighly dampened by the reasons that had prompted this topic of discussion. Visions of exhausted soldiers and smoking cannons attempted to dispel my excitement but the following announcements successfully tipped the scales. I was informed that since I carried the title of an American visitor, I would be allowed to enter the Rebbe's sanctuary for a private audience. This was a privilege I hadn't even dreamed of attaining and its actualization was as surprising as it was overwhelming. The few moments I was granted alone with the venerable leader were short but memorable and I used them to mention the names and needs of my family members.

Subsequent phonecalls and telegrams from home reminded me of the topic the Rebbe had chosen for the second maamar. My parents were frantic with worry due to the reports they were receiving from the European powder keg. The thought of war was no longer a distant haze, for it had materialized in the form of a ferocious dragon right at our doorstep. The United States consulate located in Warsaw responded to this dreaded visitor with a warning on Tuesday, August 29, that all American citizens return home immediately. They could not predict what tomorrow's day would bring and didn't want to be held responsible for the unsavory consequences.

Rabbi Jacobson left Poland that very day but the rest of us were told to ignore the dire warning. Our eyes were repeatedly drawn toward the darkening skies as pathetically out-of-date Polish warplanes valiantly practiced strategic manuevers. I wouldn't refer to the following few days as particularly peaceful ones, but neither can they be termed chaotic. Well-aware of the impending eruption, I continued to go about my cherished daily routine as if this alone would postpone the fateful moment.

Friday, September 1, 1939, successfully healed me of the last vestiges of the ostrich syndrome. My head was rudely jerked out of the sand by deafening explosions and their horrific consequences. The day had started calmly enough with a cloudless sky and mild sunshine. Following the example of most yeshiva students, my American colleagues and I had spent the long Thursday night delving into the immeasurable depths of the Talmudic seas. When the sun's rays playfully strolled across our open seforim, we reluctantly returned to everyday reality.

Two of my friends headed towards the yeshiva to learn a shiur on Chassidus before shacharis, but the rest of us decided to remain in our seats for a short while longer and review the lesson in preparation for the morning prayers. I distinctly recall the feelings of satisfaction and fulfillment while drinking my morning cup of steaming coffee. The hours of invigorating study had only heightened my desire to continue doing the same in an atmosphere so conducive to spiritual pursuit. A glance at the clock informed me that it was already 8:15 A.M. and there wasn't much time remaining before we had to leave to yeshiva. Firmly pushing away the unfinished cup of coffee and my pleasant thoughts, I focused on the printed page lying before me.

My attention was once again interrupted by the disturbing sounds of airplanes streaking across the sky. Gripped by an inexplicable feeling of foreboding,I got up to inspect the source of the disturbance, followed closely by my three companions. Six winged vehicles were flying speedily overhead like infuriated seagulls. The organization and orderly formation were apparent even from afar, and the superior workmanship of the aircraft production did not escape our fearful gaze.

"Judging from the sturdy build and neat alignment, these monsters must belong to the Germans," one of my companions commented humorously.

Chuckling over the intended barb aimed at Poland's poor military efforts, we returned to our studies. Unfortunately, the innocent joke soon blew up in our faces. A deafening explosion rocked our building and shattered its windows. I glanced at my friends in speechless horror as desperate screams tore at our hearts. Neighbors started running blindly to the basement, trying to drag their little children to safety. Paralyzed by a chilling fear, we remained in our seats, only to be bombarded by two additional explosions.

Fire-engines sped by, their revolving lights reflected on the shattered remains of what used to serve as windows. Cries of pain and injury mingled with the helpless sobs of bereavement and completely destroyed our battered self-control. Bewildered by the horrendous chain of events, the four of us made our way to the Rebbe's home for advice. As we approached the unshakeable island of calm amidst a raging sea of violence, we met some of the younger students emerging from the yeshiva building.

"Come on! Were you really scared?" they exclaimed upon seeing our whitewashed faces.

"It was only a practice exercise conducted by the Polish government. They just wanted to test the readiness of the population's civil defense. Judging from your response, this exercise was sorely needed!"

The students' patient explanation didn't allay our fears and we proceeded into the lobby adjacent to the Rebbe's study. Obviously, we were not the only people who sought refuge in the proximity of this Torah giant. The room was crowded with many Chassidim and their families but no one was given permission to enter the Rebbe's sanctuary at this difficult time. When one of the secretaries opened the door of the study, my eyes met the warm gaze of the illustrious tzaddik and I immediately felt a small measure of comfort course through my trembling being. A few moments later, the gabbai came over to Berel Levy and myself with special instructions. The Rebbe wanted us to run over to Rebbetzin Shterna Sara's residence and reassure her that there was nothing to fear. (She was the Rebbe's mother.)

I was relieved to be given clear orders at a time when clarity was a privilege of the past. Berel and I hurriedly made our way to the Rebbetzin's home with the message of reassurance. The streets were thrown into chaotic mayhem, as injured men, women and children turned to the local hospital for emergency treatment. Wagons carrying wounded people to the primitive hospital traveled alongside vehicles transporting corpses for immediate burial. Parents bemoaned the critical condition of their children while inconsolable orphans called for their mothers and fathers incessantly. The streets absorbed mountains of pain and anguish without flinching, but our hearts were incapable of accepting the scene of mourning.

A walk that usually lasted a only few minutes seemed to stretch into eternity. I felt encapsulated in a glistening, meaningful tear that represented the losses of our close-knit community. Every step we took uncovered yet another tragedy until we finally arrived at our destination. At the entrance to the Rebbetzin's building we met my brother, Shlomo Zalman, and his wife, Chaya. They, too, lived in that house and they willingly accompanied us to her apartment. Our message noticeably calmed her down for the unexpected bombings had thrown her into a state of panic. Berel and I exited the building, leaving Shlomo Zalman and Chaya in the Rebbetzin's apartment.

We returned to our lodgings and tried to make sense of the bizarre happenings. Our first step was to place a call to the United States Consul in Warsaw to find out whether war had been declared.

"I believe that this is only an attempt to intimidate the Polish people so that they would agree to Germany's demands. In the meanwhile, just listen to the radio. If necessary, I'll have instructions broadcast in English for the American citizens."

Slightly relieved, we hurried to yeshiva in a vain attempt to dress this eventful Friday in some semblance of normalcy. We had barely arrived, when Zorach Gordon placed another phone call to the American consul and received quite an unsettling report.

"Germany just issued an official declaration of war. I strongly advise you to travel immediately to Warsaw and we will arrange your return to safety."

There was no time to allow the devastating news to penetrate for the ticking of the clock had become our merciless opponent. We had to depart from Otwock as quickly as possible since failure to do so would result in fatal consequences. Necessity forced us to firmly freeze our churning emotions, as we returned to our apartment. It was time to pack up the home we had established with so much hope and enthusiasm.

Escape

Our belongings were dutifully placed in suitcases, and the widow carefully packed up adequate provisions for the Shabbos meals. The apartment assumed the impersonal look it had worn upon our arrival, and we felt like strangers in our own home. We called taxis for the journey and, in the short span of time remaining, we tried to get an audience with the Rebbe.

At about 12:30 P.M. we entered the study where the Rebbe was sitting regally, already dressed in his silk Shabbos garments. The words he told us prior to our departure were meaningful and encouraging, giving us the strength to overcome all unforeseeable obstacles.

"I think you should go to Warsaw for the time being. You should realize that all this is a test. The Torah states, 'And he saw the place meirochok, from afar'. The word 'meirochok' is missing the letter 'vov'. This indicates that when one is not far off (from accomplishing one's Divinely given task), the Satan comes and makes it into a further distance (merchak).

"You should be aware that every movement of a Jew is beloved in Heaven. Your coming here from America and your departure -you should know that it is beloved in Heaven. All this is 'because Hashem is testing you' (Devorim 13:4).

"I am sending you to my Chassidim in Riga, Latvia – but without confusion or emotional excitement. Reb Mordechai Chaifetz will make arrangements for you for nigleh and Chassidus.

"I don't know when I will see you. I am wishing you a k'siva vachasima tova and a g'mar chasima tova. May Hashem help that we should meet again in good health.

"May Hashem bless you with success in material matters and spiritual matters, and may you be yirei shamayim, Chassidim and Torah scholars."

The heartfelt words imbued us with strength and courage for whatever lay ahead. Overwhelmed by the string of blessings, we answered "Amein" in unison and got ready to exit the Rebbe's study for the last time.

Before we walked out, someone asked with obvious concern, "Rebbe, what will happen if we have to transgress the Shabbos?"

The question was asked by one but pertained to all. We waited anxiously for an answer, although we knew that our escape to safety was halachically legitimate in view of the approaching danger.

"The merit of the two great tzaddikim whose birthdates are on Chai Elul – the Baal Shem Tov and the Alter Rebbe (R' Shneur Zalmen, founder of Chabad), is sufficient that you will not need to transgress this Shabbos."

The soothing answer left no room for further talk and we slowly stepped out into the warm sunshine. Three taxis awaited us patiently at the curb, with our luggage already neatly stacked inside. When we had arrived seventeen memorable days previous, our group had consisted of six members. Upon departure, we numbered ten people for Avrohom Barnetsky and Dov Ber Levy had followed us to Otwock a few days after we arrived, and Shlomo Zalman and Chaya had decided to accompany us to the safety of home.

Approximately an hour was spent in the claustrophobic confines of the crowded taxis as we journeyed to the United States consulate in Warsaw. We sat in thoughtful silence, trying to digest our sudden transformation from serious yeshiva students to escaping refugees. Friends and acquaintances had been left behind, as well as a treasured atmosphere of Torah and Chassidus. The future was still shrouded in a cloak of uncertainty and we hoped that it wouldn't be blackened by the soot of war.

At 2:00 P.M., the three cars pulled up in front of an impressive building in Warsaw. We had arrived at the American consulate, the embassy that had promised to deliver us to safety. Confidently ascending the steps and entering the building, we allowed Shlomo Zalman to act as our spokesman. He explained to the consul that since we were all United States citizens, we expected their help in reaching Riga, Latvia as soon as possible.

I wasn't too concerned with the consul's response for he had faithfully promised to assist us when we had spoken to him earlier in the day. The answer we received rudely awakened me to unfriendly reality.

"Why didn't you leave when we told you?" the consul thundered furiously. "Didn't we warn you that war was gonna break out and you've all got to get out of here?"

We stared at his infuriated face in open-mouthed wonder. Where was the soft-spoken, controlled individual we had spoken to over the phone? How had his earnest promises and sympathy evaporated so quickly? When I thought about his strange behavior, I realized that there was only one acceptable explanation. The consul had spoken to Zorach Gordon, who possessed an obviously New York accent. This must have led him to believe that the people in question were Americans like him who simply wanted to return home. Our Jewish appearance surprised and enraged the biased official and twisted his features into a portrait of hate.

"Now you expect me to help you?" he continued loudly. "I'm getting out of here myself and I sure ain't gonna bother with any Jewish vermin! So just get out of here fast!"

His maniacal screams reverberated along the polished floors, its mocking echoes resounding in our ears. There was no way we could accept his refusal for without it we were helpless. How could ten American citizens find their way in a foreign country that had just gotten embroiled in a serious war? We pleaded and begged but our words didn't seem to penetrate his thick skull. The only method remaining was serious threatening, but that, too, proved to be useless.

"We'll have to report your inhumane treatment to your superiors in Washington," Shlomo Zalman intoned severely.

"If you don't get out of here this minute," the demon shrieked, "I'll call the police on you for trespassing!"

The nasty official would have continued hailing curses and anti-semitic slogans at us if he hadn't been interrupted by the drone of German warplanes. We were uncertain which was more destructive as we dejectedly left through the doors that had presented our only hope. It was already 4:30 when we emerged from the building, but our adventures were far from over. I began descending the wide steps, wondering what our next step would be, when the German bombs started falling all around us.

Panic-stricken, we raced back into the consulate and took shelter in the well-lit lobby. Since we were strangers in the city, we had absolutely no clue as to the locations of the air-raid shelters. We stood in the large room and murmured chapters of Tehillim with colorless lips and trembling hands. The knowledge that a stray bomb could convert this imposing structure and all of its visitors into ashes, spread a thick, somber atmosphere all around us. Tefillas Mincha was recited with the utmost fervor and devotion as we placed ourselves completely in Hashem's hands. Our situation had seemed bleak and hopeless but our fiery prayers infused us with the belief that we were not alone.

After an endless, tense hour, the neighborhood was blessed with an eerie silence. Its inhabitants hesitantly emerged from their shelters, afraid of the destruction that would greet their eyes. We emerged from the building with an inaudible song of gratitude in our hearts at our miraculous survival. To our surprise, we were met by the irate taxi drivers who had waited at the curb for our return. They demanded hefty payment for the hours they had spent in the Warsaw streets while we pleaded for our lives. We paid them handsomely and then watched them unceremoniously dump our luggage on the sidewalk and drive off.

'Where could we go now? It's almost Shabbos and we are stranded in an unfamiliar city without a roof over our heads,' I thought despondently.

Meir Greenberg, one of my companions, suddenly remembered that the Rebbe had given him a message for R' Yaakov Gourarye, a prominent Chassid living in Warsaw. Maybe he would provide a solution for our dilemma. Shlomo Zalman accompanied Meir in a taxi to R' Yaakov's house while the rest of us stood guard over our precious possessions. It was already 6:00 P.M., an hour before Shabbos, and we were still homeless in the unfriendly Warsaw streets.

I watched the hazy colors of dusk slowly assume the dark robes of night without any signs of my brother's return. An almost full moon stared down at us with eerie indifference, illuminating the deserted streets with silvery slivers of light.

"Excuse me," a passerby called in our direction.

"Yes?" we inquired suspiciously.

Experience had taught us that the Polish citizens were not particularly concerned with our welfare and any excess contact could only be detrimental.

"You probably don't know that the police imposed a strict curfew after 9:00 at night. Any groups found outside after that time will find themselves behind bars without any polite questioning. I just figured you might want to know about that."

The man waved jauntily and continued on his way, unaware of the seeds of panic he had sown in our tired minds. A visit in the Polish prison cells was the last thing we needed in our precarious situation. Every passing minute heightened our extreme tension and multiplied the suspicious sounds our imaginations perceived. It was already 7:30 and there was still no sign of our two emissaries. Had they lost their way? Did R' Yaakov Gourar-yeh have the ability to revive our shriveled hopes?

At last, Shlomo Zalman and Meir returned, breathing heavily. Their explanations came in breathless gasps as they tried to allay our fears. R' Yaakov had phoned various hotels in search of available rooms. His efforts were eventually crowned with success a few short minutes before Shabbos. Unwilling to desecrate the holy day, Shlomo Zalman and Meir couldn't ride back to the consulate. Instead, they had to find their way through the twisting streets without any assistance. From time to time, they encountered individuals who seemed friendlier than the average Polish peasant and they asked for directions. After many wrong turns, they finally met a young Jew who agreed to accompany them to their destination. Thus, long after Shabbos had spread its tranquil wings over the bustling metropolis, our two couriers had finally returned to their impatient companions.

55

56

On the Run

After we had received a detailed account of Shlomo Zalman's and Meir's adventures, we proceeded to arrange our housing for the next twenty-four hours. Meir walked back to the Imperial Hotel with his young tour guide to ascertain how many rooms were available. He returned shortly with the information that only five of us would be permitted to stay there overnight. Shlomo Zalman and Chaya would take one room while Berel Levy, Mordechai Fisher and I would occupy the other. Five of us had already found shelter in our unhospitable surroundings, but there remained an equal amount who still had no roof over their heads.

"Get out of this yard already!"

The enraged voice interrupted our careful calculations and drew our attention to a burly figure standing on the steps of the consulate.

"Don't you know what time it is? I'm locking the gates and you had better be outside with all your luggage before I have to remove you by force."

The supervisor glared at us with unconcealed disdain, deriving great satisfaction from our shocked silence. Under his watchful gaze, we dragged our suitcases out of the courtyard. The five of us who were destined to stay at the Imperial Hotel wasted no time in transferring our weary bodies and personal belongings in that direction. I plodded along the Warsaw streets, wondering what awaited us at our temporary quarters. Fortunately, the city was encircled by a kosher eiruv that permitted us to hold onto our precious possessions.

Upon arrival to our destination, we were led to two rooms, adequately clean and furnished. I started hanging my clothes in the closet, finding unimaginable pleasure in this mundane task. It was nice to be preoccupied with trivial concerns after having spent so much time in search of shelter. My friends were busily arranging their own packages and a feeling of serenity slowly seeped into our tired beings. Putting my hand in my pocket as habit dictated, I realized with a start that my passport had disappeared. A quick reckoning reminded me that I had left it downstairs at the check-in desk when we had arrived.

Taking the stairs two at a time, I hurried over to the dimwitted secretary and asked for the document. While he took his time rummaging through the untidy stack of papers strewn across the desk, I glanced at the man standing behind me. His appearance was obviously Jewish and when our eyes met, he seemed relieved.

"Good Shabbos!" he said joyously. "Are you part of the American group from Otwock?"

"Yes, I am."

I couldn't imagine how a Warsaw resident knew my identity and why he was visiting a hotel on Friday night. His subsequent explanation cleared up the matter and shed some light on the plight of my five stranded companions.

"I'm a representative from the American Joint Distribution Committee in Eastern Europe. I found your friends standing in the street with their luggage and they informed me where you were staying. Presently, I'm trying to arrange for their suitcases to be allowed into your two rooms for otherwise they will be stolen even before the clock strikes midnight."

The man tried to convince the hotel owner to accede to his request, but to no avail. There was no way to change his determined decision and the Joint representative offered a feasible alternative. He suggested that all ten of us regroup in the Hotel Britannia where there were enough rooms available. Shlomo Zalman and Chaya, followed by Berel, Mordechai, and myself dutifully replaced our clothes into the battered suitcases and once again stepped out into the unfriendly night. We were reunited with the others and without excess talking, we proceeded on our way.

It was already 9:30, a half-hour past curfew and our illegal group of eleven fearfully tiptoed through the streets. We hired a pushcart owner to transport our bulky packages, increasing the size and noise of our little tribe. The streets were still teeming with people but an eerie silence replaced the usual noise. Tramcars rode back and forth as if the curfew didn't exist, but their headlights were not turned on. Thus, black forms rode alongside shadowy silhouettes in the supposedly deserted streets of Warsaw, while we tried to find a place to spend what remained of the holy Shabbos.

Six of my companions sat in the pushcart, while the rest of us followed in groups of three. Shlomo Zalman, Mottel Altein and the Joint representative went first, with Meir Greenberg, Yitchok Kolodny and I close behind them. We had been walking quietly for several minutes when I noticed that the group we were following had turned right, but the pushcart owner had simply continued straight ahead.

'He must be a thief! That mongrel is walking off with all our possessions and no one even realized. He must be stopped!' The thought rushed through my mind with searing clarity and I immediately rushed to inform the Joint representative. Without further ado, the courageous man rushed after the disappearing figure while I returned to my two companions. We figured that Shlomo Zalman and Mottel were still waiting where the representative had left them and tried to find our way to the same spot. Yitzchok went first, but his efforts met with failure.

The Joint representative had rushed off in pursuit of our fortunes, Shlomo Zalman and Mottel had mysteriously disappeared, and a strict curfew forbade our standing around in the streets. These three discouraging facts painted a dismal picture, leaving us with no choice but to follow the path of the thieving pushcart owner. Stifled by the unrelenting darkness, we wandered disconsolately along the deserted streets. We met a young man smoking a cigarette and politely asked for directions to the Hotel Britannia. To our surprise and relief, the bareheaded young man answered us in a rich, fluent Yiddish. He led us directly to our destination in exchange for an exorbitant price, of course.

Our entrance to the hotel elicited exclamations of relief from the rest of our group. They had anxiously awaited our arrival with fervent prayers for our well-being. The innocent pushcart owner carried our luggage into the lobby and parted from us amicably. It was already 10:30 P.M. when we merited our miraculous reunion, but our troubles were far from over. Breakfast, the first and last meal we had partaken of on that fateful Friday, was eons away, as our gnawing hunger testified. We hadn't prayed the traditional Shabbos tefillos and kiddush had not yet been recited. Desperate for some semblance of normalcy in our overturned existence, we tried to rush through the necessary preliminaries before being shown to our rooms.

"Just sign these forms, please," the hotel owner requested.

We glanced at each other in consternation. What were we supposed to do in such a situation? Refusal to sign the documents would prevent our finding shelter for Shabbos, but the other option appeared impossible to carry through. How could we so blatantly transgress the holy day after all our sacrifices to retain its sanctity?

"Listen here, if you don't sign I'll have to send you out of the building."

The non-Jewish owner couldn't understand our obstinacy despite our attempts to explain the reason for our refusal. A heated

discussion ensued concerning the halachic ruling for our complicated situation. The streets were unquestionably dangerous due
to the imposed curfew and the dreaded possibility of German
bombs. Our lives would be in danger if we didn't sign the forms,
and this gave us definite permission to transgress the Shabbos.

Shlomo Zalman adamantly expressed his disagreement. The
Rebbe had promised us that we would not have to transgress the
Shabbos under any circumstances and there was no reason to
doubt his word. My brother's staunch decision convinced us of
its validity and we proudly gathered our bags for another venture into the black inkwell of a Warsaw night. Our unshakeable
faith in Hashem and His tzaddikim soon produced a miracle in
the slight form of a religious Jew. Upon hearing about our dilemma, he offered to find accommodations for us in a small, ramshackle guesthouse a short distance from the Hotel Britannia.

We followed him to our next station which proved to be
more rundown than we had imagined. Benches served as beds,
tables, and chairs, for they were the only pieces of furniture in
the shabby rooms. It was past midnight when we entered our
new quarters, and the sparse furnishings seemed like majestic
thrones. A roof over our heads, no matter how many holes and
cracks it boasted, was more valuable than comfort and pleasure.

The Friday night prayers assumed a deeper meaning when we
were finally privileged to recite it in relative peace. We fervently
made kiddush and partook of the festive meal that had been
kindly prepared for us by the widow in Otwock. Our joyous
Shabbos meal furnished the repelling surroundings with an inexplicable aura and beauty, unfamiliar in this non-Jewish area.
Stretching out on the rough surfaces of wooden benches, we
were privileged to enjoy approximately three or four hours of fit-
ful, uncomfortable slumber. We drew solace from the knowledge
that upon awakening we would be greeted by friendly sunshine
instead of the depressing darkness that had been our unwanted
companion throughout the harrowing experience.

Daylight did indeed pull us out of the blessed land where fantasy and reality are deceivingly intertwined, and we walked over to a nearby shtibel for the morning prayers. A feeling of dread welled up in us when we heard the weekly Torah portion being read. War had just been declared and the ominous tochacha in that week's parsha, Ki Sovo, seemed to indicate gruesome developments. The congregants couldn't help wondering what horrors an uncontrolled army of ruthless murderers would inflict on our long-suffering nation.

After the uplifting Shabbos services, one of the congregants announced that anyone who wished to partake of a sumptuous seuda was cordially invited to his wedding hall. He had been planning to cater the wedding feast of a couple getting married that night, but now it seemed that the wedding plans would not proceed as planned. Wasting such large quantities of food would be a shame, so he magnanimously offered it to the congregation as a gift.

I was overjoyed at this unexpected invitation, and I saw the same exuberance expressed in my friends' tired eyes. Dingy rooms and an inadequate amount of food were not very tempting after a long, sleepless night, and the unidentified caterer had made an offer we couldn't refuse. We followed our benefactor to a beautiful, spacious wedding hall and tried to enjoy the abundant delicacies. The food was delicious, as was the service, but we couldn't rid ourselves of our niggling doubts. Would we manage to escape the blazing European inferno without being injured by its merciless heat? Would the warring nations allow ten American Jews to escape their grasp?

An Uneasy Shabbos

The Shabbos meal passed in relative silence as we morosely contemplated the unusual and disconcerting circumstances. After establishing residence in the friendly Otwock environs, we had become accustomed to the fact that an endless stretch of blue-green waters separated us from our homes. Presently, seated around the perfectly set tables in a Warsaw wedding hall and partaking of an unknown gentleman's generosity, we felt decidedly uncomfortable. Home as we had known it in America seemed to be persistently distancing itself from our groping hands. The home we had recently become acquainted with in Poland had also joined the annals of history, leaving us stranded in the devastating loneliness of no-man's land.

"I'm glad to see that you managed to obtain sufficient amounts of nourishing foods. After all, you'll need all the strength you can muster to face the uncertain future."

I abruptly turned my head towards the owner of the familiar, friendly voice. The Joint representative had not forgotten about us. His genuine concern and unlimited understanding lifted our fallen spirits and dispelled the gathering clouds of gloom. Feeling like a group of young toddlers lost in the forbidding darkness, we were overjoyed to encounter anything that was even slightly familiar.

"Now, my American friends, it is time to proceed with the

planning of your escape," he said as soon as we had finished bentching.

"You want to reach Riga, Latvia as soon as possible because that country is still blessedly uninvolved in the war. In order to obtain entrance into this safe haven, we'll have to arrange visas for all of you."

We nodded in affirmation, wordlessly thanking this angel in human form for carrying the responsibility of our safety on his broad shoulders. The bright sun glared at us mercilessly as we walked toward our temporary, unpleasant quarters. Upon entering the crumbling hovel, we crisply informed the sleepy attendant that our stay had officially come to an end and proceeded to remove our various bundles and packages. Since we were headed to the Latvian embassy to get our passports stamped with a legitimate, official visa, we were certain that we would not be returning to these miserable rooms. Our suitcases seemed to grow heavier and bulkier with the passage of time, and we tried to minimize the amount of luggage we had to carry around. Thus, dressed in layers of clothing with warm, padded winter coats buttoned on top, we started our trek toward the embassy.

I felt the sun's rays roasting each layer of clothing individually and then transforming me into a melting fudge pop. Our wintry getup was not exactly appropriate for the summer heat, and therefore earned us many curious stares. Feeling ridiculously conspicuous, I followed my tired friends across the length and breadth of Warsaw in search of the desired destination.

"Here we are!" the Joint representative announced cheerfully. "Leave your packages on the steps and just follow me. We'll have you settled on the Riga-bound train in no time."

Infused with hope and faith, we raced up the steps and confidently approached the metal door. We pushed and heaved, repeatedly twisted the doorknob, and even knocked on the small glass window, with no results. The blank metal face glinted menacingly in the midday sunlight, consistently resisting our desperate attempts. I heard the thud of our spirits as they dropped down to the ground, evaporating into intangible clouds of vapor. The Latvian embassy was closed for the day and our passports remained bare of the necessary stamps.

I slowly stepped away from the entrance and picked up my scattered pieces of luggage. They seemed to weigh more than all the Warsaw office buildings put together. The top button of my winter coat audaciously popped off and went rolling down the street with careless abandon. I watched its speedy journey with exaggerated interest, following its route until it disappeared under the wagon of a passing peddler. Shlomo Zalman stood behind me with the other members of our group, trying to salvage what remained of our shattered hopes.

"It seems that this path is closed to us," our kindly guide said matter-of-factly. "I'll have to find an alternative. I want you all to give me your passports and I'll see what can be done."

We dutifully extracted our valuable documents and handed them over to our dedicated benefactor. He assured us that there was nothing to worry about and, with a cheerful wave, disappeared in the crowd of pedestrians. 'Maybe he'll meet my missing button along the way, and then they'll arrange our visas together,' I thought wryly. A none too gentle poke disturbed my whimsical ruminations and made me aware of our inconvenient location. Gathering our belongings for the umpteenth time, we retraced our steps to the dingy guesthouse and shamefacedly reregistered under the apathetic gaze of the same sleepy attendant.

Our return was well-timed for a few minutes later we were able to catch a minyon for mincha at a nearby Gerer shtibel. The soothing words of prayer calmed our rising panic and reinforced the fact that it was still Shabbos. Our feelings of rejuvenation tripled when we saw the beaming countenance of the Joint representative. He had discovered where the consul resided and personally walked over to his house with our passports. After a considerable amount of persuasion, the understanding officer stamped our passports with the long-awaited visas. The stage was set for an immediate escape.

As soon as Havdala was recited, we rushed over to the train terminal to catch the first possible ride to Riga. Understandably, we were not the only people seeking to escape the ferocious flames. The terminal was crowded with men trying to maintain a façade of serenity and confidence; with women nervously clutching bundles of food and clothing; and with young children strangely subdued due to the unusual, frightening situation. A babble of voices washed over our tired beings in tidal waves, leaving us weak and exhausted. We dropped our luggage on the platform and promptly converted them to makeshift pillows and mattresses. Sleep was the easiest solution to our present dilemma and we tried to use its services to the utmost.

Our obviously Jewish appearance combined with our apparently weakened condition made us an easy target for the rabidly anti-semitic Poles. Distinguished looking military officials revealed their true peasant origins when they bumped into our sleeping forms. I became immune to the frequent kicks and derisive laughs generously contributed by those present. The word "zhid" was usually followed by an unintelligible string of curses that heaped insults upon our innocent heads. It was fascinating to note that even in such perilous times, the crude Gentiles were still occupying themselves with illogical, uncivilized outbursts toward their Jewish counterparts. Despite the unsettling whispers of war and death, they were only concerned with degrading their hated enemy.

Hours passed in this unbearable manner until we finally boarded a train at 5:00 A.M. We were actually traveling to Riga, where we would hopefully find emotional and physical refuge. The continuous clacking of the wheels was comforting in its colorless monotony and we gratefully settled down for an uneventful journey. The events of the past few days should have warned us that any happening would be fraught with danger and surprise, but we willfully ignored that pessimistic prediction. Denial does not change reality and an unnerving announcement at 2:00 Sunday afternoon drove home that point.

"All passengers should remain seated. The train has been forced to stand still due to a German air-raid. Once again, I ask all passengers to remain seated."

The conductor's dry announcement shot a coal of fear through each crowded vehicle. We watched with horrified interest as the primitive Polish warplanes tried to combat the advanced Luftwaffe monsters. The outdated models were no match for the Germans' ruthless machines, as was evidenced in the ensuing battle taking place directly over our heads. After a few tension-filled moments, the conductor announced that the coast was clear and our journey resumed. Every few hours, similar occurrences forced us to stop short for indefinite amounts of time. Our uneventful journey had turned into a fraying string of danger and fear, sabotaging any attempts at peaceful slumber.

When the train finally crossed the Lithuanian border, we heaved a collective sigh of relief. The tumultous war zone was now safely behind us and the light of security beckoned from afar. Early Monday morning, we reached Riga, Latvia's capital city, where we were greeted by scores of concerned Lubavitcher chassidim. Upon our belated arrival, they vied for the privilege of hosting an American chassid for the duration of our stay. To settle the matter, lots were drawn and we each followed our respective host through the streets of Riga.

R' Yitzchok Kromnikov, my kind and generous host, made me feel right at home with his unlimited hospitality and warm personality. His wife, son and two daughters did their utmost to ensure that my stay was as comfortable as possible under the circumstances. The first thing we did after getting settled into our new homes, was send a reassuring telegram to our worried parents in New York. The message was short and terse, but it served its purpose.

> *Riga, September 4, 1939*
> *Agudas Chabad*
> *Arrived safely Riga out of danger. Rabbi well Otwock. Three* Hechts, Barnetsky, Levy, Kolodny, Gordon, Greenberg, Fisher, Altein.

I blissfully breathed the air of freedom and safety, promising myself that I would never again take this blessing for granted. Matters were still tense and unsteady but for the time being, my friends and I were settled in a haven of security. We enthusiastically returned to the studies that had been interrupted by our hasty flight, remaining in the Lubavitcher shul of Riga for many long hours.

Respite in Riga

Our stay in Riga was peaceful and enjoyable. The Lubavitcher community welcomed us warmly, giving us the opportunity to continue our studies with utmost fervor and concentration. I distinctly remember the Yomim Noraim in the Lubavitcher shul, where I was privileged to stand beside an unusually devout Chassid, R' Itche der Masmid. Rosh Hashana and Yom Kippur found this exalted personage praying with unparalleled devotion that seemed to form a straight path toward their destination on high. Standing in such close proximity to R' Itche provided me with the true definition of a servant of Hashem.

After Rosh Hashana, one of my American friends, Mordechai Fisher, sent a letter in Hebrew to Rabbi Shmuel Levitin, a renowned Lubavitcher Chassid living in New York, who served as a head mashpiah in the centrel Lubavitcher Yeshiva from 1940 until his Peturah.

Wednesday,(of the week) of the Torah portion Zos Ha'brochoh (7 Tishrei)

Our Rebbe, shlita, sent us to Riga and told us, before we traveled from Otwock to Riga, 'Mordechai Cheifetz will make arrangements for you for nigleh and Chassidus' (in those words). He blessed us with a g'mar chasima tova, saying that 'May Hashem help we should meet again in good health'. He explained to us how even the fact that our Torah studies have been disturbed is an act of the Satan, because he had observed how we had pressed ahead and overcome all our trials until now, and, therefore, he goes even further against us. Consequently, we have to overcome etc.

Since the Rebbe, shlita, told us all of the above and we haven't yet heard from the Rebbe, shlita, that we should travel to America, and since we too want very much to stay here as long as we can in order to fulfill our purpose for which we came here (to Europe) originally, therefore, the Chassidim here are not telling us to travel (back) unless we ourselves wish to travel. If we decide to stay, they will do whatever they can that we should (be able to) stay, and that we should lack nothing.

Therefore we have decided (except for Zorach Gordon one of the original six boys from America) to remain here at least until after Succos. Until after Succos, arrangements have been made for our study of nigleh and the yorei shamayim, R' Yitzchok Masmid, will teach us Likkutei Torah, and in the evening another Chassid will teach us a chapter of Tanya (every day).

May Hashem help us to be able to stay here in calm and tranquility.

The letter outlined our plans for the foreseeable future and we settled down for a lengthy, fulfilling stay. Mordechai had written at length the reasons for our decision to remain in Riga despite possible danger of war, and in addition to that, we all sent a brief telegram to Rabbi Jacobson to inform him of our plans.

Safe quiet here. Staying over holidays. Then will see.

Three Hechts, Greenberg, Barnetsky, Kolodny, Gordon, Altein, Fisher.

Yom Kippur was an experience that made all the rigors of our journey from distant Otwock recede from our memory. An atmosphere of such elevated piety and purity was not so easily found in any community dotting the Jewish map.

The Yom Kippur fast had obviously taken its toll on R' Itche der Masmid since he had not stepped away from his seat in shul throughout its duration. Thus, when night's comforting darkness announced the conclusion of the holiest day of the year, I breathed an audible sigh of relief. R' Itche would now be able to gather some of his usual strength and vigor with a warm, nourishing meal. To my utter dismay and astonishment, the contents of his dinner plate were nowhere near adequate. A small piece of challah and some stewed fruit were the sum total of this pious man's meal after a long, difficult fast. These were the giants of the Riga community and these were our undisputed heroes during those tumultuous times. Distant threats of a bloody war could not shake them from their usual tranquility, thus spreading a communal blanket of serenity over the immediate area.

We reveled in our peaceful world until after the first days of Succos. During chol hamoed, we knew that the time had come to move on. The precarious situation in Europe was worsening from day to day, and we couldn't afford the possibility of being trapped in its ruthless claws. Thus, we once again packed our bags and set out on a journey. Motzei Shabbos found us on the deck of a small ship heading to Norway. A trip that was supposed to take a few short hours was considerably lengthened due to a tempestuous storm at sea. Unbearable feelings of seasickness washed over us in waves almost as threatening as those on the stormy Baltic waters. When the ship finally docked at the shores of Norway, we could only hope that we would manage to disembark without tumbling down the swaying gangplank.

Tired and confused, we stood on the dock, waiting for deliverance.

"Excuse me," a polite voice interrupted our whirling doubts.

A middle-aged man approached us cautiously, motioning to some of his cronies to join him. He appeared harmless, and we could see his obvious fascination at the sight of ten Jewish passengers standing helplessly in a foreign land.

Without warning, the man reached out and lifted my hat. He peered at me in surprise and inexplicable disappointment. After courteously extending his hand in welcome, he retraced his steps and disappeared from view. His bewildered friends stared at us intensely before following their leader.

"What was that all about?" I asked in bewilderment, clutching my hat tightly with both hands. I was not ready to risk a repeat performance until I understood the significance of what I wore on my head.

"Don't you understand?" one of my friends replied with a chuckle. "These men were simply trying to find our Jewish horns. They probably never saw a real specimen in the past few decades and our arrival presented the perfect opportunity to satisfy their burning curiosity."

We laughed at the absurdity of the situation while firmly gripping our hats to prevent any additional overtures of friendship. Carrying suitcases and packages, we eventually found our way to the train terminal. An uneventful ride brought us to Stockholm, the capital city of Sweden, where we were met by Rabbi Yisroel Yaakov Zuber, a well-known Lubavitcher Chassid. His position as Rabbi of the Orthodox Jewish community in Stockholm enabled him to find accommodations for our exhausted group without delay.

Our stay in the Swedish hotel was peaceful and we blissfully returned to our interrupted studies. Unable to obtain regular kosher meals, we subsisted on fish and biscuits, or hard tack, as they were named. The peace that had become such a luxury in the European countries more than made up for our meager meals. Throughout the few weeks we resided in Stockholm, it was difficult to realize that a serious war was being waged in Poland and that millions of our brethren were already being subjected to inhumane treatment.

In distant America, our parents and Rabbi Jacobson worked tirelessly to ensure our safe deliverance from the flames of war.

High-ranking government officials in New York and Washington were approached on our behalf until our passage across the Atlantic was successfully arranged. After nearly a month in Sweden's peaceful embrace, we boarded the S.S. Mormaxport, an American cargo ship. Our journey lasted approximately ten days and we were forced to subsist only on hard tack. Several times, we were stopped by German U-boats that threatened to capsize our unarmed ship until they realized that they were dealing with American citizens.

On Shabbos, November 4, 1939 we finally docked at Hoboken, New Jersey. Standing on American soil, we tried to internalize the fact that anti-semitism had supposedly been left on the other side of the ocean. The fumes of war slowly dissipated, leaving us in a more secure reality. Sunday morning, we arrived back home in Brownsville. It is impossible to describe the reactions of our families, friends and acquaintances upon our long-awaited return from the European fires. My parents were overwhelmed with relief and gratitude to Hashem for delivering their son back home. Tears of joy mingled with tears of sorrow as we described the plight of our brethren in Poland. Concern for their welfare mingled with relief at our escape in the first few days following our homecoming.

I was relieved to be home after our uncalled-for adventures since we had departed from Otwock. Immersing myself in my studies in Yeshivas Torah V'daas helped me deal with the biting worry about the friends I had left behind in Europe. Each passing day increased the horrors perpetrated against the Jewish communities, putting my newfound acquaintances in a desperate position atop a ticking time bomb.

As the situation worsened, Lubavitcher Chassidim from all over the world tried to secure the Rebbe's escape to safety. Pressure was placed in the higher echelons of society until the prestigious officials gave in to their request. The United States government arranged for the Rebbe and his family to be escorted to safety by the German army. The fifth day in Teves was cause for great celebration in our community for we received notice that the Rebbe had successfully reached the relative safety of Riga.

A short while after his arrival, the Rebbe penned a letter to us, the eight American students, dated 14 Teves.

…While I was enduring the siege (of Warsaw), I worried about you. Several times I asked the American consul in Warsaw if there was any news from you, for I expected that you would surely try to let us know of your welfare through the consul in order to calm me and to give encouragement to my heart that is broken and shattered from the misfortunes of the Jewish people – may Hashem have pity and mercy upon them. But you did not do so. This results from lack of feeling – the love and affection that is expected according to the teachings of Chassidus.

Only when I arrived in Riga did I learn that you had arrived home safely- "Give thanks to Hashem who is good, for His kindness is eternal" (Psalms 107:11).

This letter of gentle rebuke taught us an important, everlasting lesson. It was our responsibility to inform the Rebbe of our passage to safety, since he was a concerned father for these ten young Americans who had crossed the ocean to bask in his presence.

The Rebbe finally reached American shores on 9 Adar II, which corresponded with the secular date of March 19, 1940. The perils and rigors of a transatlantic journey were obviously increased hundredfold at a time when the entire world was busy erupting like a hyperactive volcano. Despite his exhaustion, the Rebbe did not allot any time to rest and adjust to life in America. Yeshivas Tomchei Temimim of America was founded the morning after the Rebbe reached its friendly shores, and the eight of us were privileged to serve as its first students.

69

70

The Rebbe's Arrival

Yeshivas Tomchei Temimim of America was temporarily established in the basement of a small synagogue called Oneg Shabbos. Frenzied preparations characterized the first few days of the yeshiva's modest beginnings. Benches and tables were dragged down to the basement to service the ten pioneering students. A kitchen was speedily constructed in the homey yeshiva hall, transforming a dingy cellar into a room fit for use. Rabbi Mordechai Mentlik, an acclaimed student of the yeshiva in Otwock, was chosen as Rosh Yeshiva and our small group became a full-fledged student body.

The synagogue's basement served us well for many months, until more satisfactory and permanent quarters were arranged. During the months following the Lubavitcher Rebbe's arrival to New York, groups of young men and teenagers could be seen walking purposefully toward one specific destination. Students walked in from Williamsburg, Boro Park, Crown Heights and the East Side to the Rebbe's temporary dwelling in the Greystone Hotel. It was a long, exhausting trek to the hotel located in uptown New York City — the West Side, as it is called — but the Rebbe's Torah discourses more than compensater our efforts.

Much thought was invested in choosing the location of the Rebbe's home in America. Many devoted chassidim argued that the Lubavitch headquarters should be situated in a nondescript, rural town where many great things could be accomplished for Yiddishkeit. The advantages of such a spot included the fact that there would be less distractions to deter the students and chassidim from the ultimate goal. Aside from that, the Rebbe's uncompromising views on how to transform America's Jewish population to a community of Orthodox religious Jews would not garner so much opposition and ridicule in a distant, unheard-of area.

The logical arguments were all for naught for the Rebbe could not be swayed from his original decision. He wanted to completely transform the religious topography of American society and this could only be accomplished if his chassidic movement was visible to the public eye. Settling down in a quiet town would make no impression on people not included in the Rebbe's immediate circles. Extreme measures had to be implemented in order to successfully influence the general public in the ways of Hashem.

As usual, the Rebbe's will prevailed and a home was found for the Lubavitcher community. The former residence of a wealthy doctor was purchased and renovated to accommodate our needs. Located at 770 Eastern Parkway in Brooklyn, New York, the area was definitely in full public view. Opposition struck from every conceivable and inconceivable direction, but the Rebbe was not deterred. The Crown Heights Conservative community was flabbergasted at this open display of Orthodoxy and Chassidus, and they tried to put spokes in our quickly advancing wheels.

Pressure was applied by other organizations as well, such as Boro Hall, City Hall, the local congressmen and the senator representing the Crown Heights community. Unimpressed by these attempts to disrupt his plans, the Rebbe took no notice of the general public's displeasure. Chai Elul, 5699 marked the long-awaited and much anticipated day. The Rebbe, his family, and a multitude of close followers arrived at the designated house. Before entering his new home, the Rebbe turned to the enthusiastic crowd with a story about the saintly Baal Shem Tov.

The Baal Shem Tov, the father of Chassidus, once stood before the entrance of a shul and refused to enter. He remained standing at the doorway, ignoring the wordless urging of the community that he step into the sanctuary. With unconcealed wonder and curiosity, the bystanders tried to understand the cause of his strange reluctance.

"I cannot enter the synagogue because it is full of Torah and prayer," the Baal Shem Tov explained.

The enigmatic explanation only increased the confusion of all those present. If this Torah giant knew that the shul was soaked with hours of Torah study and tefillah, why wouldn't he want to cross the doorstep? Isn't that the purpose of every shul, that it should be steeped in the holy words of Torah and tefillah?

"The shul is completely full of Torah and prayer, not allowing anyone to enter. The prayers and Torah learning cannot ascend to Heaven because they were not offered with the proper feeling and concentration. Is it any wonder that I cannot walk into this shul?"

The Rebbe concluded with a sincere prayer that the shul being established at this very moment would not be filled here below. Its prayers and Torah studies should immediately find their way up to Hashem on the wings of piety, warmth and proper concentration. The crowd responded with a loud "Amen" that encapsulated their hopes and dreams for Chassidus in America. Accompanied by music and song, the Rebbe stepped into the home of Lubavitch, marking the introduction of a new era in the history of American Jewry.

Standing amongst the crowd, I knew that the wonders I had observed in distant Otwock would reappear in all their glory. While Europe was being consumed in the merciless flames of war, a new reality was taking its place. Destruction and construction were occuring simultaneously in two distant lands, ascertaining the everlasting continuity of the Jewish nation.

The following few years actualized my thoughts with unimaginable results. I continued learning in Yeshivas Tomchei Temimim until my graduation in 1942. After leaving the warm, familiar surroundings where I had been educated in the most important aspects of life, I proceeded to make yeshiva education available for communities in various states. Many cities had never been privileged to establish a proper yeshiva despite the sizable Jewish communities residing there. Fueled with a sense of purpose and the Rebbe's strong encouragement, I pioneered this unfamiliar concept in various religious kehillos. The Lubavitcher yeshivos I established in Worcester and New Haven are still in existence today, whereas the yeshiva in Buffalo, New York has already closed down. I also served as executive director of the yeshiva in Newark for six months, until the entire operation was running smoothly and efficiently.

I got married to Libe Grunhut, to the joy of family and all acquaintances. Soon after our wedding in June of 1944, we moved to Dorchester, Massachusettes where I decided to establish my next yeshiva, offering a thorough religious education. Young and idealistic, I eagerly anticipated the long lines of parents wishing to register their sons in the first classes. After enthusiastically announcing my grandiose plans in shul, I proceeded to walk through the streets of this serene Boston suburb in search of prospective students.

It was a bright, sunny morning when I began my hopeful rounds and it was a few minutes later when I realized that it wouldn't be such a simple task. Standing before the door of a friendly neighbor, I wondered if the family boasted four or five sons that were the right age for my young yeshiva. A confident knock on the door announced my presence, and within a few seconds I found myself facing the mother of my future students.

"We don't give any donations on Sunday," the lady declared emphatically, and slammed the door in my face.

The enthusiastic speech I had so carefully rehearsed remained unsaid and I dejectedly returned to the comforts of my own home. I had never imagined that it would be so difficult to turn my dream into reality, and the realization was a dreadful shock. Feeling crushed and humiliated, I wrote a dejected letter to the Rebbe, recounting my failed attempts. 'This is no job for a Rabbi unaccepted in an out-of-town city,' I wrote. My letter clearly outlined my feelings of depression and humiliation, and I waited anxiously for an encouraging reply.

The answer I received changed my entire outlook on the difficult situation. The message the Rebbe tried to convey was that "a sense of embaressment not in its proper place is basically a sign of haughtiness and pride". I was shocked by the declaration of my grievous mistake and felt my entire disposition undergo a quick transformation. Why did I imagine that the praiseworthy endeavor of establishing a yeshiva would proceed on a smooth and easy express track? Every goal worth attaining was preceded by a path strewn with obstacles and hardships. With renewed enthusiasm, I continued working on the project, unconcerned with the public's reactions.

Twelve months of hard work, both physically and emotionally, produced the desired results. Approximately one hundred and twenty students were enrolled, forming a school with five grades. Parents were reluctant to place their children in our institution for various reasons. Many were worried that their sons would become disassociated from the general American population. After being educated between the protective walls of a yeshiva, the boys would be enclosed in a self-constructed ghetto that would preclude their mingling with non-Jewish peers. Aside from that, public school offered free education while yeshiva schooling placed a great strain on a family's budget.

Despite these misgivings, we succeeded in gathering a respectable amount of students. A building was purchased in a fine residential area and a staff of dedicated teachers was employed. Weeks turned into months as our fledgling yeshiva struck deep roots and sprouted beautifully. A successful dinner was organized at a renowned Boston hotel to benefit our yeshiva. The Rebbe's son-in-law, Rabbi Shemaryahu Gourarye, honored us with his presence, as did Rabbi Predmesky, a leading spokesman for yeshiva education in America.

As the principal of a young yeshiva, I was occupied with all sorts of problems and emergencies that kept me busy throughout the day and sometimes well into the night. Aside from that, I also served as the Rabbi of a Nusach Ari shul in Dorchester, which presented its own set of challenges and demands.

Matters were proceeding with unimaginable success, but there was one area that caused me great distress. My wife was decidedly unhappy in our little town, for loneliness ate away at her peace of mind. She had escaped from Vienna, Austria in 1939 with her parents and siblings. The Grunhut family had settled in Brooklyn, New York and established their home in its unfamiliar streets. Since we had moved to Dorchester soon after our marriage, my wife was cut off from the support of family and friends. My busy schedule kept me out of the house for many long hours, and the undisturbed quiet was her formidable foe.

Considering the situation, I realized that despite the call of my young yeshiva, my wife's happiness took priority. It was decided that I would seek a suitable position in New York before parting from the rural town we had titled home. Little did I know how speedily my search for a New York job would be crowned with success.

A Syrian Rabbi?!

Precisely a year after we took up residence in Dorchester, I found myself spending the sweltering summer months with my in-laws. The relative comfort of their apartment in Fleischman's bungalow colony was a welcome respite from the unbearable heat of our suburban home. Our decision to return to the teeming streets of New York left me stranded on an island populated by unemployed and unsettled United States citizens. I didn't know where we would live and how we would make a respectable living when our blessed summer vacation wound to a close. For the duration of our stay, I resolved to put all niggling concerns on a back burner and simply enjoy the much-anticipated vacation.

Many well-to-do Syrian Jews chose Fleischman's as their summer home, and they lived side by side with their Ashkenazic neighbors. They used the shul from 7:00 to 9:00 A.M. for the morning prayers, whereas we used the same premises after they finished davening. Mincha and Maariv were conducted in the same fashion, with the Sephardim praying separately in an earlier minyon. The two groups went about their daily routines in separate lanes, due to the obvious and not so obvious differences inherent in their lifestyles. The Sephardim had their own Sefer Torah and Chazzan, and remained strictly with their own kind.

One bright, sunny afternoon, several members of the Sephardic community approached me with an odd request.

"Rabbi, we've seen you around the shul several times since your arrival. Do you speak English fluently?"

I couldn't fathom the meaning of their inquiries, but their earnest expressions convinced me that the matter was not simple chit-chat.

"Yes, of course I speak a fluent English. Is there anything I can assist you with?"

"Actually, we were wondering if you could honor our community with a speech in English on Shabbos afternoon," one man requested matter-of-factly.

I was flabbergasted by the unexpected appeal. Since my arrival at the small bungalow colony, I had come to realize that an unbridgeable gap separated the Sephardim and the Ashkenazim. There was no animosity involved, yet the two groups were too different to even entertain the possibility of sharing anything more than a friendly greeting. Why would they want a Lubavitcher chassid to speak to their Syrian community?

After considering their request, I readily accepted the formidable task. I believed that with the proper words and intentions, I could add meaning and depth to their religious observance. The Torah is universal, providing the basis of everyday life for Ashkenazim and Sephardim alike. Although I was completely unfamiliar with their mentality and lifestyle, I figured that when discussing Yiddishkeit, such concerns were insignificant.

Thus, I found myself standing at the pulpit 3:00 P.M. Shabbos afternoon, with a Sephardic audience numbering about 50 men and women. The words seemed to speak themselves, infused with passion and conviction. I felt the positive vibes emanating from those present, adding strength and power to the concepts I wanted to convey. After the lengthy, spirited address, I felt simultaneously exhausted and exhilirated. Respected members of the community congratulated me on the inspiring messages and immediately offered me a job in the Syrian community for the upcoming year.

The mere thought of serving as the Rabbi of a Syrian community seemed preposterous, and I didn't think it would come to fruition. A short while after my maiden address to the Sephardim, I was asked to speak for their Syrian friends in Bradley Beach, N.J. There, too, my words gained widespread acclaim and appreciation, leading to the realization of the unlikely idea.

Isaac Shalom, the president of the Sephardic community, visited the Lubavitcher Rebbe to inquire about my suitability for the job in question. Based on my previous experience with establishing new yeshivos in various cities, the Rebbe gave his complete consent. He reassured Mr. Shalom that being an aspiring student and successful entrepreneur, I would lead their community to greatness.

In October of 1945, I was officially nominated as the Rabbi of Bnai Magen David, a beautiful Sephardi shul in Bensonhurst. The impressive synagogue was constructed in 1922, and is still standing proudly in its original location. When I accepted the job, the shul housed a Talmud Torah, a synagogue, and a mikveh. I was employed as the Rabbi for the Sephardic youth and as the director of the Talmud Torah. The irony of the situation didn't alleviate my anxiety and apprehension as I took my first steps in an unfamiliar world.

I signed a contract for one year, which entitled me to one hundred dollars a month. Twenty-five dollars was my salary for servicing the youth and the other seventy-five was payment for supervising the Talmud Torah. Our first floor apartment, situated over a fruit store, was nicely furnished and suited our needs. The stage was set, and I nervously prepared to act as the main character. My only problem was that the script was written in a foreign language that seemed completely indecipherable to an American-born, Ashkenazi chassid. How could I begin the performance if I didn't even know how the curtains were supposed to be drawn?

My audience was well-aware of the interesting situation. The elders in the community were understandably a little uncomfortable with my position. Syrian immigrants who had paved a comfortable path in the American country were not familiar with the customs and traditions of other Jewish communities. An unfamiliar young man had been introduced as their new Rabbi, yet his background couldn't have been more different than theirs. Not only was I an Ashkenazi and a Lubavitcher Chassid, but I also carried the title of a born and bred American citizen. Unlike the traditional Sephardic Rabbis, I was not a chazzan, a mohel, or a baal korah, and I was also extremely young, to boot. The Arabic language sounded like unintelligible gibberish to my ears, and my Hebrew didn't meet the expectations of the older generation. Every aspect of my education and lineage was cause for comment and discussion since it was the polar opposite of the people I would be leading.

Throughout the first few weeks of adjustment and acclimation, I strongly identified with my name. 'Avrohom, your name is an appropriate description of your feelings and experiences,' I told myself wryly. 'Avrohom Avinu stood on one side and the entire world and its inhabitants strongly opposed him. You should be thankful that your congregation is doing its best to understand and welcome you in their midst. The present difficulties won't last forever!' The words of encouragement worked wonders during those trying times, despite the fact that I was the only one uttering them.

My first public address to the congregation stressed the verse "Kee anashim achim anachnu" – because we are all brothers. I wanted to emphasize the fact that although I wasn't proficient in their language, customs, and lifestyle, we were still brothers. Our backgrounds differed greatly, yet we were still members of the same family. Boruch Hashem, the speech went over very well and the message I wished to convey was understood and accepted.

The job I had accepted presented many unforeseen challenges that demanded endless work and tireless efforts. The years 1944 and 1945 marked the return of countless Syrian youths who had served in the American army. Years of gruesome combat, unpleasant company and non-Jewish surroundings had taken their toll on the spirited young men. Many had forsaken the ways of their ancestors in favor of the unshackled, gilded lifestyle they had observed in the army barracks. Others were traumatized and depressed by the gruesome sights of bloody battle. Their lives seemed meaningless and worthless despite the absence of ammunition, uniforms, and shrieking air raid sirens.

I had to ignite the dormant sparks of Torah and Yiddishkeit that had been smothered by the clouds of war. Hours of preparation went into each speech, lecture and class that was relayed to these searching young men. Eventually, their regular attendance at prayers and functions increased dramatically, in direct proportion to their renewed interest in Judaism. A large room was set aside on the upper floor of the Bnai Magen David building to service the young congregation. During the Shabbos services, the number of young men attending reached astronomical heights of four hundred, and sometimes even five hundred, members. Their progress was often painstakingly slow, but the occasional spurts of interest and enthusiasm added bursts of color to the overall picture.

76

Setting a Standard

Raised in the streets of New York, I understood the needs and desires of the returning soldiers. The topics and discussions that would interest them were not foreign to me, and I therefore managed to garner their trust within a comparatively short while. Simultaneously, I had to direct my attention to the second facet of my position.

The Talmud Torah offered its fair share of difficulties too, in those first years. The yeshiva had been established with shaky foundations, since the Sephardic Rabbi presiding over it was ill-equipped to deal with American-born children. He was not familiar with the English language and did not understand the needs of the young generation. Therefore, the Talmud Torah was headed for failure under his auspices. When I got acquainted with the unappealing state of affairs, I understood that drastic measures had to be taken in the right direction.

In the morning, our student body consisted of young boys in kindergarten. They were too young to attend public school as their older siblings did, so they merited an untainted Jewish education for one year. When I arrived in the Syrian community, there were only two classes of kindergarten children, Class 1A and Class 1B. With great toil and effort, the student body expanded dramatically, forming six classes instead of the previous two. The conditions in the classrooms were nothing to take pride in, for no one had seen the importance of providing the necessary furnishings and decorations.

I realized that emergency funds had to be procured in order to raise the standards of our pre-school education. The New York Board of Jewish Education had been established a few years previous, and I decided to try my luck in that direction. Government funding for Jewish schools was unheard of in the 1940's but I figured that our school qualified as a first experiment. After countless pleas and endless cajoling, my request was met with success. Two thousand dollars, quite a princely sum in those days, was poured into the Talmud Torah's empty coffers. The money was used to purchase sorely needed tools and furniture that helped our rooms assume the appearance of decent classrooms.

In the afternoon, from 3:30 to 7:30, the yeshiva hosted its second set of students. This group was much larger than the first, for it included all the boys who attended public school throughout the day. After long hours of study in the secular environment, the rambunctious young boys made the effort to attend classes more suited to their special status as Jewish children. From their earliest years, the Sephardi children were trained to value their Torah studies and everyday tefillos. The boys were expected to read fluently at the mere age of five and were regularly taken to the prayers in shul. Even during selichos, the prayers recited in the early morning hours thirty days before Rosh Hashana, Sephardi fathers brought their youngsters to shul. Thus, the young children were accustomed to praying with a large minyon on a daily basis.

Until today, these grown-up youngsters harbor an outstanding respect for Torah and tefillah b'tzibur. When moving to a new neighborhood, their first concern is the proximity of a proper shul and yeshiva. Concepts ingrained in young minds remain fixed for eternity.

The afternoon studies in Bnai Magen David was no simple

matter and demanded extreme concentration. When Chumash was taught, the boys weren't told the explanation in English. Rather, they had to contend with a translation called Sharach – an Arabic translation of the Hebrew words. The American children were unfamiliar with the language of their Sephardi ancestors and therefore found the words difficult to understand.

In contrast, the Yeshiva of Flatbush taught everything in English. The students understood what was being taught, and were able to relate to their studies. Bnai Magen David had to contend with the stiff competition offered by the Flatbush yeshiva. It was a daunting challenge but the Syrian community accepted it with determination. At present, the Yeshiva boasts an extensive student body numbering more than eighteen hundred members. There are also many young yeshivos, offshoots of Bnai Magen David, that service the members of the Syrian community.

The responsibilities involved in running a youth group and an expanding Talmud Torah were numerous, yet I enjoyed the challenge. There was much to be done for the five hundred families of my Syrian congregation then and I felt honored to serve as their leader. Some characteristics of the flourishing community fascinated and interested me as an American, Ashkenazi Chassid. Religious Sephardi professionals were an impossibility at that time. Lawyers, doctors and accountants were not available in our community because anyone going for a college degree almost automatically discarded his religious upbringing.

At present, the Sephardi community in America is comprised of nearly eighty thousand people. The boys learn in Magen David Yeshiva and continue their education in theit own High School Yeshivot and Kollelim. Sephardi girls are now Yeshiva High School graduates, a reality that couldn't have been more distant in the mid-1900's. The term "religious, Sephardi professional" is no longer a paradox, since there are many young men who aptly fit that description. As I had observed in the over fifty years that I had served as the Sephardic Rabbi, the Syrians have been blessed with a healthy and flourishing community that holds onto the traditions and minhagim of their ancestors. Several yeshivos for girls are presently enjoying great success in their expanding enrollments. Many graduates become teachers and profesioals who are totally observant members of the community.

Flatbush Feud

The years passed slowly, allowing me to acclimate to my unfamiliar neighborhood. Congregants who had spoken a foreign language and followed strange customs appeared more understandable and approachable. I mastered an understanding of the Arabic language, an accomplishment that made it possible to forge relationships with my Sephardi neighbors. Long nights and mountains of effort formed a smooth road for my developing community.

After several long years, the strange puzzle pieces were finally beginning to fall into place. A picture of striking beauty emerged in the form of a sturdy link in an everlasting chain. The Sephardi youth enthusiastically followed their ancestors' example, carrying their Jewish badge with pride and devotion. Their growing interest and the increasing number of students marked the success of the Talmud Torah.

In the years of 1946 and 1947, a number of experts were called down to our developing yeshiva. Their complimentary reports gave us the impetus to continue with our monumental work.

Dr. Noah Nardi, the Educational Consultant of the Jewish Education Committee of N.Y., visited our facilities and sent me a report of his favorable impressions.

"The school on the whole has made considerable progress," he wrote. *"The classes are well organized and the teachers are*

competent…The whole atmosphere of the school – the joy with which the children pursue their studies, makes indeed worthwhile all efforts and sacrifices which you and your committee are making towards the building up and the development of the only Sephardic Yeshiva on the American continent."

We also invited Rabbi Chaim Karlinsky, the Educational Supervisor of the United Yeshivos of America. He wrote a letter stating that "in the last six months, the Yeshiva has made giant strides ahead and the pupils have succeeded exceptionally well in their studies."

The effusive praise our young yeshiva garnered from professionals in the field of education, spurred us on to continue expanding and advancing. Yeshivas Magen David eventually developed into a modern, established school that serves the Syrian community faithfully until the present day.

My position as the Rabbi of a Sephardic community had already become part and parcel of daily existence. Complicated matters and initial misconceptions had already been resolved, yet a spark of trouble appeared from an unexpected direction. A Jewish developer who had already established several nursing homes was planning to build a health-related facility. A home for the mentally challenged was definitely a commendable project, but its planned location was a disastrous choice. The developer wanted to build the facility on Ocean Parkway and Avenue F. Ocean Parkway was the home of the thriving Flatbush community. Real estate value was quite high and the residents were Jewish families who appreciated the quiet and safety of a civilized neighborhood.

The establishment of a health-related facility would destroy a flourishing community in the name of altruistic goodwill. Workers employed at the home would represent all faces of society, including many undesirable elements. Their presence in a predominantly Jewish neighborhood would be detrimental to the quality of life desired by its residents. Homes would be rented and sold to nurses, janitors, and personal aides. It would be impossible to screen their characters, so Flatbush could easily be transformed into a crime-infested society. Respectable Flatbush residents would slowly move out of these unsavory neighborhoods, bringing an abrupt end to a beautiful community.

How could I sit with folded hands when a flourishing, praiseworthy community stood precariously at the brink of collapse? Establishing a facility for the unfortunate, mentally-ill American citizens was a commendable enterprise, but we didn't want it in our own backyard. I knew that these plans had to be opposed, yet no one seemed too concerned with the disastrous ramifications. The Rabbinical Board had no qualms in rebutting my passionate pleas for action. Disappointed and surprised, I went down to the local planning board and voiced my thoughts.

"I believe," I thundered dramatically, pointing my finger at the chairman of the board. "I believe that you have been convinced to remain silent by the developer's glittering thousands!"

My words caused an unprecedented uproar in the quiet offices of the local board. One man literally attacked me, but I refused to retract my offensive comment.

"And for that matter," I continued relentlessly, turning to my violent attacker. "I believe that you can be accused of the same underworld crimes."

The staid, shocked audience simply gaped in shock at my audacity, but the point had been made. A shadow had been cast over the supposedly sterling characters of the project's supporters, and I readied myself to continue the one-man battle on other fronts as well.

My Syrian congregants couldn't begin to understand why I was wasting my time and energy on these protests. Originating from lands where their lives were led peacefully and calmly, they were not used to getting involved in community affairs. They described me as the "crazy rabbi" who busied himself with all sorts of projects for the good of the public. Although they found my efforts interesting, they were not ready to lend their support and understanding. I tried to drive home the fact that my work was geared for their benefit, for if the facility was established in Flatbush, the effects could reach our community.

Matters were begging to be settled, and my efforts started snowballing at an unexpected speed. A woman residing on Ocean Parkway, a mere two blocks away from the facility's planned location, called me up in a state of uncontrolled panic. After hearing about the site for the undesired establishment, she realized that her property value would drop dramatically. Real estate values of the Flatbush neighborhood were fated to decrease significantly if the project would merit seeing the light of day. A practical discussion brought us to the understanding that an organization would have to be founded to counteract the developer's persuasive millions. Rather than having several one-person attempts to stop the approaching monster, we would combine forces to form a unified group.

Thus, the Flatbush Community Council was formed, at the impetus of an inconsiderate developer. My organization included Jews as well as non-Jews residing on Ocean Parkway, who were concerned about the undesirable transformation destined for their calm, civilized community. I contacted all the synagogues while the Gentile woman publicized the venture amongst her circles. Public meetings were held and flyers were distributed to publicize our intentions.

Perturbed by our serious attempts to disrupt his plans, the developer sent several rabbis to meet with me. They were supposed to convince me to drop all charges, in exchange for a monetary bribe. My son-in-law would be given a job under this man's auspices, and he would earn $15,000 a year. I was disgusted by the underhanded methods employed to purchase my silence, and repeatedly turned away the developer's messengers.

"Why don't you accept his proposal? You'll earn the long-awaited peace as well as your son-in-law's financial security!" one rabbi earnestly said.

My reply was swift and unhesitating.

"I'm sorry, Rabbi. I really don't want any dirty money," I said emphatically, firmly showing the man to the door.

The battle raged for years, and no one seemed to be gaining the upper hand. I suggested that the developer choose a different location for his laudable project, but the wealthy man adamantly refused. In the early 1960's, the dispute was brought before the City Planning Commission. It seemed that the developer managed to obtain permission to proceed with the construction, but I was not willing to surrender. Flatbush would not be brought to an early death if I could prevent it.

My next step was to involve the entire community in my never-ending efforts. Many rabbis addressed their congregations and informed them of the terrible fate awaiting their flourishing community. Simultaneously, Catholic priests described the situation to their Gentile followers, gathering their unanimous support.

We organized several well-attended puplic meetings that met with great success. The developer realized that we were a force to be reckoned with, so he tried enlisting the assistance of the Lubavitcher Rebbe. After explaining his position and the obstacles I was placing in his path, he begged the Rebbe to influence me to drop all charges.

"Why don't you go to a Din Torah?" the Rebbe inquired calmly.

The disappointed developer left the Rebbe's study with the bitter taste of defeat lingering in his mouth. He never called me to any Din Torah, for he obviously knew who would be proven correct. How could one compare my battle for the Klal to his selfish desires?

86

87

88

89

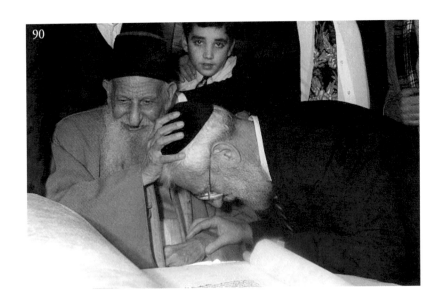

The Battle of Ocean Parkway

While the determined developer was campaigning for the right to establish a health-related facility on Ocean Parkway, trouble was brewing in different areas as well. The City Planning Commission decided to extend the Brooklyn-Queens Expressway through Ocean Parkway. Buffeted by these tempestuous waves threatening to drown their beautiful ship, the Flatbush community didn't know what to do first. An increased crime rate and decreased real estate values sneered from one side, whereas pollution, noise and constant traffic roared menacingly from the other.

I continued organizing public meetings and mass rallies to fight for the survival of Ocean Parkway. Accompanied by several prominent community representatives and a group of one hundred and fifty concerned civilians, I made my way towards Borough Hall. We wanted to speak with Sam Leoni, the Borough President, in order to gain his support and advice, but the matter was not so simple. Sam Leoni refused to step out and face our insistent demands, but we were not easily deterred.

"Come out, Sam Leoni," we cajoled. "Don't be a coward! Come on out and show your face!"

The Borough President surrendered to our willful demands and agreed to meet with us. Words were thrown through the air like ping-pong balls, but nothing much was accomplished. The institute for mentally-ill adults was fated to strike its roots in the heart of Flatbush and the Brooklyn-Queens Expressway was destined to do the same.

The chairman of the City Planning Commission, a young man by the name of John Zucatti, urged me to raise the white flag of surrender.

"Rabbi Hecht," he said earnestly. "We're going to build that health-related facility on Avenue F."

"You most definitely will not!" I retorted hotly.

Zucatti was surprised at my steadfast determination and proceeded to display his own will of iron.

"We'll see about that," he said smugly, insinuating that my tireless efforts would never reach the ladder of success.

"I'm ready, Mr. Zucatti. The battle is on!"

The irate chairman glared at me with unconcealed hostility. He was not accustomed to being crossed by anyone, and certainly not by an ordinary American citizen.

"Listen to me, Rabbi," he proclaimed ceremoniously. "You just can't fight City Hall!"

He turned away brusquely, convinced that the argument had been resolved.

"Well, I've got news for you," I called out resolutely. "Not only am I going to fight City Hall, but I'm also going to beat that invincible, august institution!"

I was determined to carry out my confident declaration, although the task seemed close to impossible. Our growing organization, the Flatbush Community Council, continued its display of defense and resistance. I knew that the developer's plans and the dreams for the expanding the Brooklyn-Queens Expressway could only become reality with the approval of the City Planning Commission, which included the five Borough Presidents and the mayor.

The City Planning Commission had already voiced its unanimous approval, but we could still exert our influence over the other two sides of the powerful triangle. Thus, I went to visit each of the Borough Presidents and clearly explained the basis of our opposition. The mayor, too, merited a visit and a passionate plea for understanding and assistance.

One wintry Friday morning, I was driving along the peaceful streets of Ocean Parkway with my son, Eli. The car rolled smoothly along the paved streets, while my thoughts tumbled over each other in an unrelenting maze of confusion.

'How could the developer dream of disrupting this beautiful community?' I wondered. 'And doesn't the City Planning Commission realize how a busy highway would damage the face of Flatbush?'

My melancholy ruminations were rudely interrupted by an unwarranted commotion. I nervously turned the corner to discover the source of the noise, fervently hoping that my suspicions would be proven groundless. Unfortunately, the sight that met my eyes confirmed my thoughts. A large, monstrous tractor gleamed menacingly in the cold glare of the winter sun. Its jaws devoured mounds of cement in mere seconds, leaving destruction in its wake. Construction for the health-related facility was obviously underway, despite the fact that permission had never been granted.

'Construction or destruction?' I thought wryly.

I wrathfully parked my car directly in front of the forty-foot pit that had been formed by the tractor's ruthless movements. The dark hole appeared to me like a mass grave for the Flatbush community, spurring me on to take immediate action.

"Mister!" I called out furiously to the shocked driver of the tractor. "You'll have to drive over me and my children if you want to continue your destructive work."

The burly man gaped at me in obvious surprise, leaning precariously out of his seat to get a better view.

"Rabbi, are you nuts?" he inquired, none too politely.

"No, most definitely not!" I replied indignantly. "You are just not allowed to do this!"

Our verbal combat escalated and intensified with each passing moment. I refused to move away from the large pit, while the driver insisted on continuing his work. At last, I had the police called in, and they effectively diffused the tension. The construction worker was dutifully informed that without a permit, his work was considered illegal. As I watched the tractor disappear around the corner, I proceeded to run the errands I had set out to do several hours earlier. Erev Shabbos preparations pushed the disturbing incident out of my mind for the time being, but I realized that the latest development could not be ignored. Pressure was building from all sides, but I could not allow the developer to be crowned as the victor in our long, drawn-out dispute.

The tension took its toll on my health, and I was forced to take a short vacation in Florida. The short break did wonders for me, but I couldn't bear to stay away for too long. I knew that matters were proceeding rapidly back home in New York, yet I didn't know in which direction the winds were blowing.

As soon as I returned home, I was greeted by a public gathering with nearly fifteen hundred participants. The massive assembly was an expression of the community's interest and support in the project I had undertaken on their behalf. Several weeks after the successful gathering, I organized a different sort of protest. Our next attempt was titled "The Baby Carriage Brigade" and it merited a lot of publicity.

One hundred and fifty women lined the streets with carriages and strollers. They wanted to emphasize the fact that a busy highway or a health-related facility would disturb the peaceful atmosphere so treasured by the Ocean Parkway residents. Traffic was held up and pictures were taken, and then the strange rally was disassembled. Our original idea had definitely made an impression on the important, respected personalities we wished to persuade.

It wasn't long before a meeting was arranged to make a final decision. The City Planning Commission, five Borough Presidents, and the mayor gathered at 10:00 a.m., at City Hall. Opinions were voiced and ideas were proposed, yet nothing was unanimously accepted. The meeting lasted for approximately thirteen hours, until 11:30 p.m.. At last, when the hands of the clock slowly ticked their way towards midnight, a decision was made.

The developer's plan was outvoted, and the Brooklyn-Queens Expressway suffered the same fate. Ocean Parkway had been saved after many years of tireless efforts and unimaginable pressure. I exulted in the knowledge that my hard work had not been for naught. The flourishing Flatbush community had been given a new lease on life, which I hoped would extend as long as necessary.

Nowadays, when one strolls down the quiet streets of Ocean Parkway, it is difficult to imagine the threats that nearly disrupted its peaceful existence. One would be hard-pressed to picture what the neighborhood would look like if a highway was built through its center or if an influx of questionable characters would flood its streets.

World Battles

Victory had been achieved, but the work had not come to an end. The congratulatory words of John Zacatti resounded merrily in my ears as I proceeded to solidify our present success for future Ocean Parkway generations.

"Rabbi, my compliments to you," the chairman of he City Planning Commission said sincerely. "We had a great battle and you won hands down. You beat the city!"

I had defeated City Hall, but I knew that the tables could be turned at the slightest provocation. There were no guarantees that future developers or highway fans would not vanquish our unprotected community. This logical line of reasoning prompted us to campaign for the continued safety of Ocean Parkway. After applying pressure in the right places, our efforts bore fruit. Ocean Parkway was officially listed as a "historical landmark". The precious landscape of Flatbush could not be altered in any significant manner without explicit permission of numerous high-ranking officials.

Many years later, R' Moshe Sherer of the Agudah wanted to establish a senior citizens' home on Ocean Parkway. He applied for a permit and received a surprising reply.

"You had better approve this venture with Rabbi Hecht," he was told. "If Rabbi Hecht approves it, you may proceed with your plans."

Of course, I readily agreed to the Agudah's plans, for a Jewish senior citizen's home posed no threat to our community's survival.

Another challenge I was faced with in my fight for Ocean Parkway's survival was a law that had been passed many decades previous. According to the law, shuls or yeshivos were not allowed to be constructed anywhere along the length and breadth of Ocean Parkway. I protested the unfairness of this law and met with the committee several times to clarify my viewpoint. Congressman Stephen Solarz assisted me in this particular campaign and, with his help, the law was speedily annulled.

In 1974, I tried to prevent the establishment of a public high school on Avenue K, but I was unsuccessful. The public school had been situated on Ocean Parkway for many years without causing any undue aggravation. In the 1970's, the Board of Education decided to build a high school on a site adjacent to the elementary school's location. I wouldn't have taken a stand on this latest development if the future students would have been our cordial Gentile neighbors. To my consternation, I was informed that only five percent of the North Central High School student body would be residents of Ocean Parkway. The remaining ninety-five percent would be bussed in from East New York.

The Board of Education wanted to integrate the schools from several different neighborhoods, so they came up with a complicated zoning plan. Most of the students attending any specific school would be residents of different areas. I was concerned with the strange elements that might be imported daily to the new high school on Avenue K. How could we allow absolute strangers with questionable backgrounds to populate the schools in our vicinity?

Aside from that, I was also worried about the location of North Central High School. The school was established in close proximity to the Yeshiva of Flatbush, and I feared possible friction and strife between the two culturally estranged groups.

Being a man of action, I immediately contacted the powers in command. To my extreme consternation, my numerous letters could not stand in the path of the quick-paced machine. The Board of Education was determined to actualize its plans despite my vehement protests. My efforts, though, did have some effect. The percentage of students bussed in from other areas was greatly reduced, as stated in a letter I received from Phillip Groisser, an officer at the Board of Education.

"…Under the plan, admission priorities make it possible for over <u>fifty percent</u> of the student body to be taken directly from the Flatbush community…

"I know you will be pleased to hear that Mr. Saul Bruckner, former head of the Social Studies Department of John Dewey High School, has been elected as principal of North Central. He is a superior educator with all the necessary qualifications to make the school an exemplary educational institution. Mr. Bruckner is eager to work cooperatively with the community, so that pupil and community needs are met most effectively."

Problems cropped up along the streets of Ocean Parkway like mushrooms after a rain, but their solutions usually sprouted soon after their appearance. While I was battling energetically at the home front, serious battles were being conducted in other parts of the world.

In June of 1967, the advanced Israeli Air Force completely demolished and obliterated the Egyptian Air Force. The fearless Israeli pilots had destroyed the entire fleet of advanced warplanes while they were still stationed unsuspectingly on the ground. The stunning victory excited the Jews living in Israel and enraged their Arab neighbors. Within minutes of the unprecedented defeat, the entire Middle East was sizzling with exhilaration and anger, with pride and absolute shame. The steaming cauldron on the other side of the Atlantic sent little puffs of smoke to our stable Syrian community in New York.

When I heard the astonishing news, I realized that the unexpected victory could have severe repercussions. The Arab countries were so enraged by their ignominious defeat that they would definitely not allow it to pass in silence. Jewish communities under their domain would suffer as a result of their leaders' public defeat.

I was concerned that the Jewish communities in Aleppo and Damascus, Syria would be tortured and penalized for the success of their Israeli brethren. The sincere worries of my community urged me to once again approach the officers who possessed the power to stem the bubbling flow of fury.

At the behest of my friend, David Cohen, I sent a telegram to Mr. George Baroudy, an Arabic ambassador at the United Nations. Mr. Baroudy represented Saudi Arabia and he possessed awesome powers of persuasion. His fluency in the English language coupled with his captivating oratorical skills gave his opinions much clout and recognition. Therefore, I requested a personal meeting with him at the United Nations to discuss the fate of Syrian Jewry.

Considering his respected position and the Arabic blood flowing through his veins, I didn't expect a positive response. The reply I received caught me completely off-guard. Mr. George Baroudy set a date for our meeting and graciously invited me to the United Nations building in Manhattan.

His unwarranted acquiescence was cause for great rejoicing amongst my Sephardic congregants. This was a golden opportunity to ensure the safety and equality of our fellow Jews who were suffering under their Arab rulers. I carefully chose several prominent community members to accompany me on the sojourn into enemy territory.

Hours were spent in endless debate. We tried to formulate our requests in a manner that would be acceptable to the Saudi Arabian representative. Ideas were discussed and discarded with alarming frequency, until we finally agreed on a basic syllabus. All that was left to do was to pray for success.

The long-awaited day finally arrived, accompanied by hammering heartbeats and trembling fingers. As I walked towards the entrance of the imposing United Nations building, I felt a heavy responsibility resting squarely on my shoulders. I heard the voices of young children calling out to me with hope and anticipation, praying for my success. If the meeting proceeded along the desired tracks, our suffering brethren could be released from potential danger.

I glanced at the expressionless faces of the policemen who had been sent to guard us until we reached our destination. They seemed unconcerned with the outcome of our meeting, as did the sentries stationed along the corridors of the large building. Their apathy did not surprise me. After all, only a Jewish heart has the ability to transcend all distances in sympathy for the plight of Jews worldwide.

98

101

102

103

104

At the United Nations

We were solemnly ushered into a large, brightly illuminated meeting hall. Mr. George Baroudy greeted us warmly and then introduced us to the other members of the Arabic delegation. After several polite handshakes and practical smiles, it was our turn to announce our names and positions.

I cleared my throat importantly and plunged into a fabricated rendition of my Syrian ancestry. At a convention consisting solely of Arabs and dealing with the safety of Syrian Jews, I couldn't introduce myself as an American citizen who essentially had no connections with Syria at all.

"I am the oldest son of Chacham Ibrahim. My father, may his memory be blessed, was the spiritual leader of the Syrian community for many long and fruitful years."

I spoke in fluent Arabic, thus causing those present to accept my imaginary lineage without any reservations. I swallowed a smile as I watched them nodding their heads in acceptance of my respected position.

The delegates looked at me expectantly, waiting for the inevitable requests for peace and security. Aware of their unwillingness to extend any assistance to the lowly Jews, I kept my requests very simple.

"You are all representatives of different Arab countries," I stated confidently. "I strongly urge you to convince the govern-

ing bodies in your countries to place the entire Jewish population in Syria under the protection of the Red Crescent."

The Red Crescent is an organization operating in the Middle
East that carries the same responsibilities as the Red Cross in
America. If the Syrian Jews would be placed under their protec-
tive wings, their future would be stable and secure.

My audience didn't erupt into an uncontrolled, explosive
shouting match as I had feared, so I immediately voiced my second modest request.

"As you know," I continued calmly. "There are numerous Syrian immigrants in North and South America who have been cruelly separated from their families back home. A lot of money and
much effort has been expended to reunite them on American
soil, but it was all for naught. The immigrants' parents and siblings cannot obtain permission to leave their Syrian homes. In
the modern, democratic world of today, how can one forcibly
separate a family unit?"

I glanced meaningfully at the delegates sitting calmly around
the table, waiting impatiently for a flicker of response. The State
of Israel had not been mentioned, nor had the Egyptian defeat
been alluded to. This was done to prove that there were no political interests tainting our views. We were not entwined in Israeli affairs, and all we requested was the safety and equality of
the Syrian Jews.

Subdued murmurs followed my passionate pleas. The Arabs
seriously discussed the modest requests I had voiced, trying to
decide on a proper response. In the interim, Mr. George Baroudy
approached me with a genuine, accepting smile. He touched my
beard and stated emphatically, in Arabic, "Ah! This Rabbi is a
true Syrian and I respect him!"

The other members in my delegation looked at each other
quizzically. They harbored no doubts about the American origins of their Chassidic Rabbi, yet this respected Arab had been
completely fooled. My preliminary words of introduction and

the fluency I exhibited in the Arabic language led the Arabs to believe that I had been raised in Syria. How were they supposed to realize that I had never laid eyes on that distant country?

After a short, earnest discussion, Mr. Baroudy agreed to fulfill our request on one condition. He wanted our Syrian Community in New York to print a full-page advertisement in the New York Times stating that we disapproved of the Israeli military operations. We would also have to express our sincere appreciation to the Red Crescent for the protection they extended over the Syrian Jews.

We mulled over the possibilities with increasing agitation. It was impossible to accede to their demands. How could a Jewish community condemn the actions and victories of our heroic Israeli brethren?

While these thoughts were racing feverishly through our minds, the Arabs displayed their impeccable manners. In a gesture of friendship and goodwill, they served us steaming cups of Turkish coffee and an assortment of sweets. The cheerful puffs of vapor clouded our view, but our decision remained unequivocal. Despite the attempts at mutual understanding, we could not accept their offer.

"We have heard your conditions, and we will consider the offer carefully. At present, we cannot give a definite reply, for we must have the plan approved by our entire community," I said politely.

Several minutes passed in amiable discussion, and the meeting was finally adjourned. We had failed to accomplish the task we had set our sights on, but the stage had been set for future attempts. Although this venture had not met with success, we were satisfied with the friendliness displayed by the Arab delegates. We had not reached an official agreement, but the altruistic intentions of our meeting did have an effect.

The Jews living in Syria informed us that after our meeting at the United Nations, President Assad issued strict warnings pertaining to all Syrian residents. The Arab population was warned against attacking any Jew or Jewish house. Such an action would result in severe penalties.

This meeting had not been the first demonstration of concern for the Syrian Jews. Thursday, November 4, 1971, the first prayer vigil for their freedom had been organized to protest the distressing news we heard. The newspapers had publicized these worrisome reports, awakening the conscience of the general American public.

The New York Times, Sunday, October 31, 1971
An appeal to the conscience of mankind
on behalf of Syrian Jewry.

Excerpts from Statement on Jews in Syria, issued by Gen. Lucius D. Clay, U.S. Army Chairman, Committee of Concern:

The Syrian authorities are holding in jail 12 young Syrian Jews, charged with having attempted to flee the country. Their names are: Isaac Hamra, his sister Charlotte Hamra. Misses Badia Dibbo, Fortuna Boukai, and Rosette Yachar; Messrs. Abdo Sadia, Nissim Bissou, Sabah Ariel, Eli Mougrabi and Azur Blanga. The last named is 27 years old and was arrested with his wife (24) and their four-year-old son. The others are all in their late teens or early twenties.

There are reports that they have been interrogated under torture, and held under strict solitary confinement. The Syrian security police have similarly interrogated the relatives of the 12 Jews and the relatives of others who have either succeeded in fleeing the country in the past or who were suspected of planning to escape.

The desperate attempts of Jews to flee the country are prompted by the cruel conditions to which the community has been subjected for years. Among the restrictions imposed upon the Jews of that country are:

A total ban on Jewish emigration or even visits abroad.

Even within Syria itself travel by Jews is restricted to three kilometers from one's home. Further movement requires a special permit which is generally not granted.

Distinctive identity cards for Jews with their religion marked in red.

A variety of economic restrictions in employment and a total ban on the sale by Jews of their houses or other real estate.

We call on the Syrian authorities to cease their persecution of the Jewish minority, to free those unjustly imprisoned and to permit those Jews who wish to emigrate to do so.

This worrisome information prompted a mass rally in front of the United Nations on November 4, 1971. It was the first of many demonstrations and gatherings that were organized for the benefit of Syrian Jewry. Although there wasn't a trace of Sephardic ancestry in the roots of my extended family tree, I felt an inexplicable affinity with the community I had learned to lead and understand.

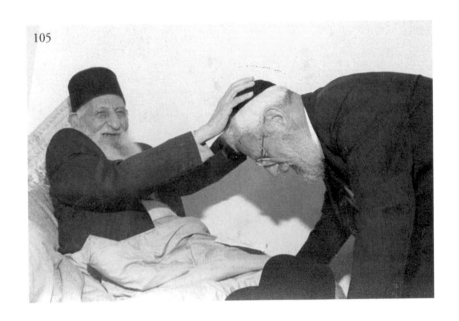

Tension in Syria

Throughout the following years, I continued to exert my influence in various places on behalf of those relatives and acquaintances of my congregants who were still suffering in Syria. I personally visited several representatives of the Arab countries in Washington D.C. to ensure that they treat their Jewish populations fairly and equally. When I tried to make contact with the Syrian ambassador, my task became decidedly complicated.

At first, he refused to meet me under any circumstances, but a fair amount of pressure convinced him to rescind his decision. When I finally managed to set up a convenient date for our discussion, my euphoria was unmitigated, albeit short-lived. We conversed in the Syrian dialect of the Arabic language, but the common language, English, was the only thing we were capable of sharing. My questions were answered very diplomatically, meaning that they were not answered at all. My attempts to extricate a promise for the security of the Jewish communities in Aleppo and Damascus met with failure, for the Syrian representative was afraid to utter any decisive comments. A slight slip-up on his part would result in his immediate, merciless execution at the hands of his barbaric leaders.

Aside from the personal meetings I arranged with the Arabic delegates, there were several additional meetings organized by a committee I participated in. Our efforts did not go unnoticed, but we weren't satisfied with partial success. The goal of transplanting all of Syrian Jewry to American shores stood tantalizingly before our eyes, repeatedly urging us to increase our efforts.

I enlisted the assistance of Congressman Stephen Solarz, who had helped me immensely in my battle for the survival of Ocean Parkway. He used his connections to initiate contact with the Syrian authorities in reference to our worthy cause. In December of 1976, he journeyed to the Middle East to reinforce the international relations of the United States. Despite the numerous issues that fought for his attention, the dedicated congressman did not forget about our ongoing mission. Upon his return, he sent me a letter detailing his journey and an invitation for a thorough discussion on further attempts.

"I recently returned from another mission to the Middle East, in my capacity as a member of the Committee on International Relations...

"I'm writing now in order to invite you to a private off-the-record briefing on the prospects for peace in the Middle East in general, as well as the status of the Jewish Community in Syria, in particular...

"I'm sure I don't have to tell you that 1977 is likely to be a year of intensive diplomatic activity in the effort to achieve a settlement of the continuing conflict between Israel and the Arabs and, if you think the members of your congregation or organization would be interested in hearing a firsthand report on the situation in that troubled area of the world, I hope you won't hesitate to let me know so that the necessary arrangements can be made."

Matters were arranged in other areas as well. We managed to wrangle permission for a few shipments of Judaica to pass the Syrian checkpoints, with one uncompromising stipulation. None of the books, seforim or siddurim was allowed to be printed in Israel, for that would be considered enemy contraband. Since most of the Judaica we had procured were Israeli products, we simply tore out the pages that stated their manufacturing location. Thus, countless cartons of soul-sustaining material made their way into the darkness of Syrian existence. The luminous, everlasting messages dispelled some of the dense fog that characterized their difficult lives in the late 1900's.

Several years passed in relative safety, until a horrendous crime exploded like dynamite. The entire world erupted in fury when they heard about the murder of a young woman and her two innocent children.

December 28, 1984:

A member of the Syrian community in Aleppo received a telephone call in his shop. An anonymous caller asked him why he was still in his shop, when he was so desperately needed at home. Confused and irritated, he continued with his work, wondering why someone would want to play such an inane prank.

Several hours later, the young man locked up his shop and hurried home. He was convinced that the queer telephone call had simply been a practical joke, yet his subconscious seemed to be whispering dark and sinister messages.

As soon as he turned the doorknob, the first hint of trouble attacked him with malice. The door was unlocked, and a deathly silence greeted him as he walked through the darkened corridor. A couple of hesitant steps brought him to a scene that would forever remain engraved in his memory with all its gory details.

His twenty-six year old wife lay motionless on the floor, in a pool of blood. His six-year-old firstborn son lay alongside his three-year-old daughter. The homey living room assumed the atmosphere of a graveyard at midnight, and he felt helpless in the face of such unmitigated horror. His entire family had been cruelly murdered, leaving him the lone survivor of a cheerful, united family unit.

Several Jewish families living in Aleppo received anonymous

threats, warning them that they would meet the same fate as the unfortunate family. The clammy hands of sheer terror gripped the Jewish residents of Syria in a viselike grip, as their lives seemed to crumble before the hands of unidentified murderers.

Safely settled in our comfortable homes in America, we were unprepared for the reports that traveled speedily over the Atlantic expanse. Our brothers in Syria were living at the tip of an overactive volcano, which threatened to put an end to their uneasy lives. I immediately sprang into action, propelled by the heinous crime that had completely eradicated any illusions of peace and security in the Arab countries.

Meetings were organized, delegations were sent, and demonstrations were held. The general public strongly empathized with the plight of the defenseless Jewish communities, and pledged their support for our cause. Armed with the knowledge that our brothers desperately needed assistance, we exerted an unimaginable amount of effort to procure their safety. I recall one convention in particular which met with marked success. Hundreds of people from Europe and South America attended that international conference in Paris, in November of 1984. In a whirlwind sequence of events, I arrived at the convention, delivered a lecture on the desperate plight of Syrian Jewry, and boarded a plane returning to America. The entire trip was squeezed into one action-packed day, but its success lived on for many long years.

The situation slowly improved, as Syrian Jews were given permission to emigrate. In the beginning of our campaign, we had to plead incessantly for the release of a few Jewish residents, but as the years passed, our efforts were crowned with success. In the years 1997 and 1998 we finally merited to reach the peak of our aspirations. The entire Jewish population of Syria, totaling approximately five thousand souls, was permitted to immigrate to the land of their choice. Majority of the Syrian Jews landed on the welcoming shores of America and were speedily included in the flourishing Sephardi communities.

It's interesting to note that Syrian Jewry was not alone in its fight against virulent anti-semitism. In 1982, we received alarming reports about the Jewish community of Tunisia. Rumors abounded, obscuring the actual occurrence, but the information we received called for immediate action. The Tunisian consulate had closed the synagogue on Yom Kippur, the holiest day of the year. Jews were barred from praying in shul, leading to burning resentment and fear. I immediately sent letters to those who could effect a change, and the situation never escalated into a serious problem. Until today, we have been unable to unearth the actual happenings in Tunisia on that fateful evening.

It had taken many decades of work, but we had finally been privileged to welcome our suffering Syrian brethren to an existence virtually untainted by anti-semitism and crime.

111

My Visit to Germany

When Chaplain Captain Martin Applebaum approached me to lead the annual Torah Convocation in Europe, I felt invigorated by the monumental task begging for my attention. The Armed Forces for the Jewish personnel in Europe organized an inspiring and uplifting convention every year, which succeeded in spreading the light of Torah to those who had not yet recognized its truth. The request to lead this incredible venture in 1981 appealed to my desire for challenge and growth. Chaplain Applebaum's detailed explanation of the responsibilities and difficulties involved in such a venture didn't impinge on my enthusiasm for the project. It was only towards the conclusion of our conversation that I was hounded by the first whisperings of doubt.

"This year's Torah Convocation will take place in Germany, so. . ."

The rest of the chaplain's sentence was lost in a haze of shock and disbelief. How could I possibly travel to a land whose streets had apathetically witnessed the murder of my innocent brethren? Was it possible to spread the light of truth in a land of such warped mentality? Mere mention of the infamous country sent shivers of apprehension and disgust rushing through every fiber of my being.

Horrifying pictures of concentration camps flashed before my eyes in full color, while heart-wrenching screams of "Shema Yisroel" resounded in my ears. I wordlessly watched blood-streaked numbers marching solemnly in an orderly line, forming the symbolic number of Jewish Holocaust victims. 'Six million of my brothers and sisters perished at the hands of the German residents,' I thought fiercely. 'It is simply impossible to ignore the nation's ignominious history.'

Captain Martin Applebaum noticed my hesitation and proceeded to offer words of encouragement and gentle persuasion. His promises of great accomplishments in the name of Torah and Yiddishkeit proved to be stronger than my natural disgust towards the German country. With the encouragement of the Lubavitcher Rebbe, I painfully swallowed one of the most difficult chunks of Jewish history and accepted the leadership of the Torah Convocation of 1981.

All preparations were speedily completed for there was barely any time at my disposal. I gratefully threw myself into a frenzy of activity, temporarily shelving my well-founded hesitation. The day of departure arrived sooner than I had anticipated, and I mechanically went through the necessary motions. As I seated myself comfortably on the monstrous aircraft, I couldn't help remembering a similar journey.

More than forty years previous, I had embarked on a journey to the European continent. I had been an idealistic young man in search of Torah and Chassidus when I had crossed the Atlantic by boat for the first time. With Otwock, Poland as my destination, there wasn't any cause for apprehension or doubt. I had known with unparalleled certainty that learning Torah in the proper atmosphere, under the tutelage of a gadol hador, easily outweighed all the efforts and difficulties our trip entailed.

Nearly forty-two years after that short, memorable journey, I was once again traversing the same path. A streamlined airplane had replaced the unpredictable, slow-moving water vessel, yet the route had remained unchanged. I thought about the difference in destinations, and a tremor once again attacked my unstable equilibrium. The atrocities committed by the Nazi party leered menacingly behind my closed eyelids, successfully foiling my plans of crossing the border to the land of blessed repose.

"I will have nothing to do with those barbarians," I decided firmly. "Germany will be my home for several weeks, but I refuse to feel comfortable in its repelling embrace. Spreading the teachings of Torah and Yiddishkeit is a noteworthy cause, and I will not allow myself to be sidetracked by anything else."

My unyielding stance lent an air of serenity and purpose to my confused thoughts, making it possible to finally enter the elusive kingdom of sleep. Although I was quite fluent in the German language, I decided not to make use of it throughout my stay. I would respond in English to any questions and queries, for I didn't want to sully my mouth with that despised language.

With roaring engines and last-minute seatbelt instructions, the large airplane landed in Frankfurt. I was supposed to catch a connecting flight to Stuttgart, Germany, where I would be met by my hosts. The short period of time I had at my disposal was spent in the airport lounge, surrounded by numerous Germans. At first, I was overwhelmed with unexpected feelings of curiosity. 'These are specimens of the superior Aryan race,' I thought cynically. 'They represent the pinnacle of human achievement and civilization.'

I glanced at the perfectly-poised men and women waiting impatiently for their flight to Stuttgart. They looked like normal human beings, without any signs of superiority to differentiate them from the entire world population. Tidbits of animated German conversation stole their way into my subconscious, reminding me of the merciless commands coolly given in Auschwitz and Birkenau. I tried to ignore the unnerving German sounds and unsightly sea of blonde hair and blue eyes, but my attempts were doomed to failure.

My beard and conspicuous black hat unmistakably marked me as a religious Jew. I felt like the proverbial sheep wandering amongst a merciless pack of wolves. The Aryan civilians seated around me appeared indifferent to the stranger in their midst, but their true feelings were anyone's guess. When our flight was finally announced, I was soaked by a premature wave of relief.

I boarded the Lufthansa aircraft along with my polite, albeit unsavory, companions. I was traveling on a German airplane, in the company of proud Aryans towards a bustling German city. Irony was certainly enjoying itself at my expense throughout the interminable forty minutes of my flight. A trusty little sefer tehillim helped me retain my sanity until I finally reached my destination.

The sight of several escorts dressed in American Army uniforms filled me with relief and renewed self-confidence. As I reveled in the sounds of a regular English conversation, I allowed myself to release some of the pent-up tension that had accumulated during the past few hours. A dazzling display of greenery and natural beauty captivated me as we drove towards the hotel in Stuttgart. I was enamored by the rustic cottages and awesome views of countryside in full bloom.

'That's German countryside you're enjoying,' I berated myself sternly. The words of description provided by my gregarious escorts wafted out of the open windows, without registering in my feverish mind. I couldn't allow myself to enjoy the beautiful view that had displayed a face of hate and distaste to my murdered brethren.

As soon as we arrived at the hotel, I was respectfully ushered into the V.I.P. suite that was reserved for two-star generals, like me. My sojourn in German territory had begun.

On German Soil

Rabbi Applebaum introduced me to the Chief of Chaplains, Colonel Harding, who was in charge of thirty-one Jewish chaplains residing in Germany. At the time of my visit, towards the end of May, 1981, there were approximately 213,000 American troops stationed in that infamous country. After an interesting conversation with the Chief of Chaplains concerning the living conditions of the American soldiers, I was taken to Major General Boyle, the commanding general of the Seventh Corps.

We were joined by General Boyle's faithful deputy, Colonel Knarowski, and our discussion assumed a very intellectual note. Their intelligence, modesty and capabilities were brought to light during the course of our conversation about the readiness and trustworthiness of the United States troops stationed in Germany. A mutual respect rested comfortably on the table between us as we concluded the impromptu meeting.

The Jewish Welfare Board sponsored a lay leadership seminar, directed by Colonel Joseph Messing, the Director of Chaplaincy of the Jewish Welfare Board of New York. I thoroughly enjoyed the week of speeches and panel discussions that characterized the seminar. When I was asked to deliver a lecture to the officers of this convention, I readily accepted the challenge. Rear Admiral Packard was taken as the guest speaker, and his presence was considered an honor. As the person who was in direct control of the American fleet in the Mediterranean, Admiral Packard was reverently titled as one of the leading officers of the Navy. His honorary status lent impetus to his illuminating remarks, which were well-received by the entire audience.

A noteworthy incident that took place during that same week was my interview on the Armed Forces Television. I spoke passionately for more than thirty minutes and my words were broadcast on German television.

"Israel was a nation long before the German Federal Republic," I stated vehemently. "Thus, we do not need Helmut Schmidt's advice or sympathy."

I discussed some of his publicly aired observations about the P.L.O. and general statements regarding the Jews and Judaism. The reactions of several citizens and government officials proved that my remarks went over well and made an impression on the many thousands who heard my words.

After a week of getting acquainted with my hosts, my new surroundings, and the general situation of Jewish army officials, I was ready to address the members of the Torah Convocation. The Convocation took place in Berchtesgaden, Austria and was attended by more than one hundred servicemen and their families. I was slightly overwhelmed by the task that loomed before me in the form of cultured European army officers, but thoughts of what was waiting to be accomplished infused me with additional sources of energy.

Words of Torah, Yiddishkeit and belief in Hashem washed over the crowd on seven different occasions, as I stood confidently on the podium. The sparkling eyes of my large audience expressed their interest and understanding in the matters being discussed. When the final session on Motzei Shabbos wound to a close at 1:00 A.M., I knew that my efforts had been well-invested. The Torah Convocation members had been inspired by the lectures and presentations, and their warm reactions helped my distaste to the host country fade into temporary oblivion.

Several days later, my initial feelings of repulsion resurfaced with renewed vigor and conviction. In the company of my new European friends, I visited the mountain hideout of the modern-day Haman. Forty years previous, Hitler had sat placidly in the Hotel Walker, stationed on an imposing mountain, and he had planned the obliteration of the Jewish nation. Consumed by an inordinate amount of hatred for his innocent victims, the demonic German ruler had proclaimed that a Jew would never dare tread on his rugged mountain.

As I felt the elevator rising quickly to that elusive mountain peak, I couldn't quell the feelings of vengeance and rage bubbling furiously through my bloodstream. I felt like I was carrying out my duties as a faithful Jew by proudly stomping over the hideout of a civilized barbarian.

"Hitler called this spot the 'Eagles' Nest' because of the fabulous view it provides," one of my companions stated matter-of-factly.

Clutching my trusty little sefer tehillim, I glanced at the miniscule towns and villages spread out below. The mountain is over 6,000 feet high and one of the highest mountains in all of Germany. Standing at the peak, one can barely make out the indistinct shapes of houses and vehicles abounding in the bustling, modernized cities. The scenic beauty is intoxicating and relaxing, infusing one with serenity and peace.

'How was it possible to concoct such a poisonous plot when surrounded by such natural wonders?' I pondered. 'How did Hitler think of horrific mass murder while he was sitting in the awe-inspiring lap of nature?'

The painful paradox simply enforces the teachings of the Talmudic sages. Through continuous work and effort, man is capable of reaching levels higher than the angels, but without the guidelines of faith in Hashem, there is no telling how low he can fall. Hitler had been fueled by a lust for power and superiority. He had brutally murdered his conscience along with the millions of men, women and children he had sentenced to death. The beautiful hideout had failed to make an impression on his animalistic desires.

I recited several psalms that tell of the ultimate destruction of all evildoers. Then I turned to those chapters that praise the continuity of the indestructible Jewish nation. Each word I uttered seemed to throw another spear at the proud Nazi ideals, transforming their Aryan superiority into a shameful mound of destruction.

Before we departed from the Eagle's Nest, I poured a soft drink into a disposable cup and loudly recited the proper blessing. The words of my fervent beracha rolled along the grassy slopes and craggy stones, bouncing proudly through Hitler's hideout. The name of Hashem had been declared in this forsaken spot as a sign of our nation's eternal life.

We quietly descended the majestic mountain in a modern, up-to-date elevator. As I walked away from the Eagles' Nest and from Hitler's nefarious hideout, I felt the sweet taste of the ultimate revenge. A group of observant Jews had proven the failure of the Nazis' Final Solution.

Inspired with renewed faith and pride in our Jewish origins, we chose our next destination. We decided to visit Dachau, the infamous death camp where approximately 30,000 Jews had met their violent deaths in the crematoria.

STEPHEN J. SOLARZ
13TH DISTRICT, NEW YORK

COMMITTEES:
FOREIGN AFFAIRS
CHAIRMAN, SUBCOMMITTEE ON ASIAN
AND PACIFIC AFFAIRS
BUDGET

Congress of the United States
House of Representatives
Washington, D.C. 20515

WASHINGTON OFFICE:
1536 LONGWORTH HOUSE OFFICE BUILDING
WASHINGTON, D.C. 20515
(202) 225-2361

DISTRICT OFFICES:
1628 KINGS HIGHWAY
BROOKLYN, NEW YORK 11229
(212) 965-5100

117 BRIGHTON BEACH AVENUE
BROOKLYN, NEW YORK 11235
(212) 965-5105

October 22, 1982

Rabbi Abraham Hecht
2110 Ocean Parkway
Brooklyn, N.Y. 11223

Dear Rabbi Hecht:

I thought you might like to see the enclosed letter I recently received from Powell Moore, the Assistant Secretary for Congressional Relations, in response to the letter I sent President Reagan concerning the situation in Tunisia that you brought to my attention.

I gather there seems to be a disagreement about what actually happened there, although I am open to any additional suggestions you might have about how I can be helpful in this regard.

Needless to say, if you believe the synagogues were closed in Tunisia during the high holidays, I believe they were closed also. The real question, insofar as I'm concerned, is what we should do about it and that's where I'd like to get the continued benefit of your thinking and advice.

I also was delighted to hear from Jackie Kassin that you'd like me to speak at the synagogue on Saturday, October 30, and I'm very much looking forward to seeing you on that occasion.

Cordially,

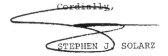

STEPHEN J. SOLARZ

SJS:cid

DEPARTMENT OF STATE

Washington, D.C. 20520

OCTOBER 7 - 1982

Dear Mr. Solarz:

I am writing in answer to your letter of September 23 to President Reagan about the closing of synagogues in Tunisia during the recent Jewish holy days.

Our Embassy in Tunis reports that the synagogues in Tunisia were open on Yom Kippur and that it had no reason to believe they had been closed during previous days.

It would be uncharacteristic of the Tunisian Government to deny its Jewish community freedom of worship or protection. More characteristic was the appeal for Jews and Arabs to work together which President Bourguiba of Tunisia made on the Islamic holiday of Id al-Adha, coinciding this year with Yom Kippur. The germane portion of his statement reads:

"In a year so overburdened with painful events which have threatened the very foundations of universal ethics, ethics which owe so much to the teachings of the first revealed religion, in this year's Yom Kippur day which coincides with the celebration of Aid El-Idha, I appeal to all Jews to work together hand in hand for peace."

With cordial regards,

Sincerely,

Powell A. Moore
Assistant Secretary for
Congressional Relations

The Honorable
     Stephen J. Solarz,
          House of Representatives.

Nazi Atrocities — Up Close

Our car traveled smoothly along the paved roads of the German countryside, making its steady way towards the horrific concentration camp. A wealth of natural beauty whizzed past the windows, sending messages of life and renewal to all who took the time to listen. I gazed in silent wonder at the fields of wheat, fruits and vegetables basking in the warm sunshine. Brilliantly colored vegetation marched in orderly rows to the horizon, disappearing modestly into the heavenly azure expanse.

There weren't any buildings to disturb the growing wonders, and we allowed ourselves to be charmed by Germany's innocent face. I temporarily forgot the gruesome sights awaiting us at the culmination of our journey, lulled into relaxed enjoyment by rural society.

A large chimney stack looming menacingly from behind a thick, fortified wall abruptly pulled me out of the induced serenity. I saw rows of barbed wire and imposing watchtower structures, and I knew that we had arrived. Dachau was comfortably nestled amongst beautiful fields and orchards, disguising its despicable colors in cloaks of green. In my mind's eye, I pictured the chimneys belching out thick clouds of black smoke. The smoke spread out over the calm, peaceful environs, bearing tid-

ings of atrocious deeds committed behind the barbed wire en-
closure.

How was it possible that the thousands of Germans who pic-
nicked gaily amongst the fields of greenery did not notice the
significance of black smoke? Didn't they realize that the cries of
pain were not a figment of their imagination? Hundreds of German civilians passed the gates of Dachau on a daily basis. How
did they explain the monstrous crematoria, the harsh-looking
sentries and the yards of barbed wire?

The Germans' insistent denial about the crimes perpetrated
under their auspices was an obvious lie. It was impossible to
believe that they had all been deaf and blind while Dachau was
transporting its prisoners to a world devoid of pain and anguish. I was amazed by the fact that an entire nation could
blatantly utter the same senseless lie without batting an eye-
lash.

The world mistakenly blames only members of the Nazi party
for the atrocities committed during the Holocaust. In truth, every civilian who resided in the accursed country during those ill-
fated years had lent a hand to the merciless killings. Silence was
their deadly weapon, and selective blindness was their ammunition. They saw the clouds of black smoke and they heard the
heart-wrenching cries of anguish, yet they chose to remain indifferent. Their apathetic attitude was as destructive as the murderous actions of the Nazi puppets.

Our car rolled to a stop before the gates of the infamous
death camp. I stepped out of the vehicle, trembling with apprehension and barely controlled fury. The indignities bestowed
upon my brothers and sisters filled my heart with a confusing
mix of anger and sorrow that threatened to explode in the heat
of the moment.

An extensive chart greeted me upon entering Dachau. It hung
conspicuously on the wall, listing all the smaller concentration
camps situated around Dachau. We had entered the mother

camp, where most inmates were processed and killed. Any extras or remnants were shipped off to the smaller death camps, where they were duly disposed of.

A large, empty area was cordoned off in the center of the camp. The ten barracks that had served as the Jews' living quarters during those terrible years had been razed to the ground, to remove the last vestiges of incriminating evidence. In their stead stood a simple marker announcing that the empty lot had once been the site of several ramshackle buildings.

I walked deeper into the camp, and met up with the symbol of barbarism. The gaping mouths of the crematoria sneered at me with typical German pride, insinuating that it never regretted the mass murder it had committed. My eyes stared into the blackness within, searching for a sign of life. I wanted to see those pious European Jews swaying calmly over their gemaras. I looked for the warm Jewish mothers cooking up a storm in honor of the Shabbos.

I strained my eyes to find images of the past, but my efforts were in vain. A vast blackness stared me in the face, quashing all pictures of a world gone up in smoke. Revered grandparents, devoted parents and innocent young children had all traveled the same painful path. Their travails had ended in a single puff of smoke that spread tales of hatred throughout the polluted German atmosphere.

With bowed shoulders and a quickened heartbeat, I walked away from the gaping ovens. Our next stop was the museum that had been erected as a memorial for the thousands who had passed through the gates of Dachau. The dreadful events were recorded in full, gruesome detail for posterity.

'Why don't you spend your vacation in this museum?' my heart screamed to the indifferent German public. 'Take one look at what your revered ancestors have done, and maybe you'll stop valuing your despicable Aryan blood to such a ridiculous extent. Where were your famous measures of modernization and civilization when these crimes were committed? Why did they choose to hibernate during those difficult years?'

Swallowing my pain, I firmly resisted the urge to flee the area. My nation had been subjected to devilish schemes, yet they had remained faithful to their Father until the very end. The least I could do in their memory was to learn about the atrocities committed against them.

I once again took out my sefer tehillim and recited several psalms. The age-old words of Dovid Hamelech reached out to me in the forsaken concentration camp, giving meaning to an inconceivable human tragedy. Songs of praise mingled with cries of pain, as I sought relief from the One who had planned it all.

Standing before the blackened crematoria, I recited the prayer of 'Kel Maleh Rachamim' in honor of the deceased. I felt powerless in the face of such uncompromising evidence, and the holy tefillah restored some of my peace of mind. The thirty thousand kedoshim had ascended to their proper places on high, and they were certainly praying on our behalf.

We walked out of the camp quietly, dragging our feet over the paved roads. The car engine disturbed the graveyard silence, pulling us back to the present. As we traveled past the beautiful fields, I couldn't hide my distaste for the German scenery. These grounds had been cultivated while my innocent brethren had been shoved into stifling barracks. German families had enjoyed their vacation days amidst a profusion of greenery, taking no notice of the screams emanating from a distant death camp.

I vowed to publicize the atrocities I had witnessed throughout the entire world. Let everybody hear about the so-called innocence of the civilian population. The cruelty of the Nazis was a known fact, yet no one had ever discussed the murderous indifference of the German citizens. Dachau's location left no doubts as to the apathy of the Nazis' anonymous assistants.

UNITED NATIONS HIGH COMMISSIONER
FOR REFUGEES

HAUT COMMISSARIAT DES NATIONS UNIES
POUR LES RÉFUGIÉS

WASHINGTON LIAISON OFFICE

DÉLÉGATION A WASHINGTON

1785 MASSACHUSETTS AVE., N.W.
WASHINGTON, D.C. 20036

TELEPHONE: (202) 387-8546

March 6, 1984

Rabbi Abraham B. Hecht
Congregation Shaare Zion
2030 Ocean Parkway
Brooklyn, NY 11223

Dear Rabbi Hecht:

Thank you for your letter of February 3, 1984 in which you raise the concern of treatment of Jews in Syria. I apologize for the lateness of this reply.

I have sent a copy of your letter to our headquarters in Geneva for their information and comment. I will contact you as soon as I receive a response from my inquiry. Please be assured of our concern in this matter. Thank you.

Sincerely,

Joachim Henkel
Acting Representative

Congressional Record

United States
of America   PROCEEDINGS AND DEBATES OF THE 89th CONGRESS, SECOND SESSION

Vol. 112   WASHINGTON, MONDAY, APRIL 25, 1966   *No. 68*

Senate

Monday, April 25, 1966

The Senate met at 12 o'clock meridian, and was called to order by Hon. ROBERT C. BYRD, a Senator from the State of West Virginia.

Rabbi Dr. Abraham Hecht, president, Rabbinical Alliance of America, Brooklyn, N.Y., offered the following prayer:

אבינו שבשמים מלך העולם

Sovereign of the universe, Almighty G-d in Heaven, may this hour be an hour of favor and acceptance in Your sight.

Our hearts are lifted unto You in gratitude for Your mercies and kindness toward the people of these blessed United States. More especially, do we thank You, O L-rd, for bestowing upon this great land, legislators and statesmen who will guide with the help of Almighty, the destiny, and stir the hearts of men and women, young and old, to serve their country in truth and loyalty.

Bless this august assembly and their families. May they be granted peace of mind, serenity and spirit, and inner tranquillity predicated upon faith and trust in G-d. May those who occupy themselves with the affairs of our country always faithfully seek Your guidance in pursuing its welfare, its advancement, its growth and security.

Pour down Your bountiful blessings upon our distinguished and beloved President, Lyndon B. Johnson, his family, and all the peoples of this great democracy, so that peace and prosperity, freedom and tolerance increase and endure throughout the length and breadth of its borders.

May we realize in our day the prophetic vision of Isaiah—LVIII—as engendered by the various programs advanced by this illustrious legislative body for the welfare of mankind.

To loose the fetters of wickedness,
To undo the bands of the yoke,
And to let the oppressed go free,
And that you break every yoke?
Is it not to deal your bread to the hungry,
And that you bring the poor that are cast out to thy house?
When thou seest the naked, that thou cover him,
And that thou hide not thyself from thine own flesh?

We pray to the Ruler of the universe that His blessing continue to be bestowed on all inhabitants of our country, that prejudice and malice be ...., that all its citizens regardless of race, color, or creed will know the joys of prosperity, tranquillity, and peace. Amen.

DESIGNATION OF ACTING PRESIDENT PRO TEMPORE

The legislative clerk read the following letter:

U.S. SENATE,
PRESIDENT PRO TEMPORE,
Washington, D.C., April 25, 1966.

To the Senate:
Being temporarily absent from the Senate, I appoint Hon. ROBERT C. BYRD, a Senator from the State of West Virginia, to perform the duties of the Chair during my absence.

CARL HAYDEN,
President pro tempore.

Mr. BYRD of West Virginia thereupon took the chair as Acting President pro tempore.

THE JOURNAL

On request of Mr. MANSFIELD, and by unanimous consent, the reading of the Journal of the proceedings of Thursday, April 21, 1966, was dispensed with.

MESSAGES FROM THE PRESIDENT

Messages in writing from the President of the United States were communicated to the Senate by Mr. Jones, one of his secretaries.

REORGANIZATION PLAN NO. 3 OF 1966—MESSAGE FROM THE PRESIDENT (H. DOC. NO. 428)

The ACTING PRESIDENT pro tempore laid before the Senate the following message from the President of the United States, which was referred to the Committee on Government Operations:

To the Congress of the United States:

I transmit herewith Reorganization Plan No. 3 of 1966, prepared in accordance with the Reorganization Act of 1949, as amended, and providing for reorganization of health functions of the Department of Health, Education, and Welfare.

Today we face new challenges and unparalleled opportunities in the field of health. Building on the progress of the past several years, we have truly begun to match the achievements of our medicine to the needs of our people.

The task ahead is immense. As a nation, we will unceasingly pursue our research and learning, our training and building, our testing and treatment. But now our concern must also turn to the organization of our Federal health ....

As citizens we are .... to the very best health services our resources can provide.

As taxpayers, we demand the most efficient and economic health organizations that can be devised.

I ask the Congress to approve a reorganization plan to bring new strength to the administration of Federal health programs.

I propose a series of changes in the organization of the Public Health Service that will bring to all Americans a structure modern in design, more efficient in operation and better prepared to meet the great and growing needs of the future. Through such improvements we can achieve the full promise of the landmark health legislation enacted by the 89th Congress.

I do not propose these changes lightly. They follow a period of careful deliberation. For many months the Secretary of Health, Education, and Welfare and the Surgeon General have consulted leading experts in the Nation—physicians, administrators, scientists, and public health specialists. They have confirmed my belief that modernization and reorganization of the Public Health Service are urgently required and long overdue.

II

The Public Health Service is an operating agency of the Department of Health, Education, and Welfare. It is the principal arm of the Federal Government in the field of health. Its programs are among those most vital to our well-being.

Since 1953 more than 50 new programs have been placed in the Public Health Service. Its budget over the past 12 years has increased tenfold—from $250 million to $2.4 billion.

Today the organization of the Public Health Service is clearly obsolete. The requirement that new and expanding programs be administered through an organizational structure established by law more than two decades ago stands as a major obstacle to the fulfillment of our Nation's health goals.

As presently constituted, the Public Health Service is composed of four major components: National Institutes of Health, Bureau of State Services, Bureau of Medical Services, Office of the Surgeon General. Under present law, Public Health Service functions must be assigned only to these four components.

This structure was designed to provide separate administrative arrangements for health research, programs of State and local aid, health services, and executive staff resources. At a time when .... functions could be neatly compart-mentalized the structure was adequate. But today .... situation is different.

Homecoming

My journey along Dachau's horrific paths caused me unimaginable pain and anguish, but several subsequent discoveries enlightened me as to the actual extent of Nazi brutality. Six million innocent souls had ascended to Heaven on the wings of German atrocity, yet the death toll was still mounting uncontrollably in the year 1981. Thousands of ignorant Jews fell unsuspectingly into Hitler's bestial trap without realizing the tragedy of their situation.

An intense and informative conversation with Rabbi Greenwald, the Rabbi of Munich, unveiled a devastating loss of Jewish identity. I learned that throughout Germany, the intermarriage rate was approximately 50%, whereas the Berlin area boasted nearly 65%. Kosher restaurants in Munich, Stuttgart and Geneva attributed their ability to continue functioning to the Jewish communities' subsidizations. No one chose to eat in certified kosher restaurants, for they saw no need to set themselves apart from their Gentile counterparts. Food that was deemed appropriate for the general German populace was perfectly acceptable and palatable for the assimilated Jews in their midst.

The Israeli owners of the kosher restaurant in Munich complained bitterly about their non-existent customers.

"How is it possible that out of a population of six thousand Jews, only one or two customers should frequent our establishment?" the distraught owner exclaimed pathetically. "Why would survivors of the Nazi war machine willingly step into the arms of their sworn enemies?"

I mulled over his anguished queries, feeling their piercing points puncturing my heart. It was truly unbelievable that Jews were still blindly following their civilized Aryan neighbors towards their own self-destruction. Apparently, the Holocaust that had claimed so many of their innocent brethren had failed to make an impression on their assimilated views and fickle desires. A drunken stupor is sometimes easier to disturb than the deep sleep of a wandering Jewish neshama.

Rabbi Greenwald continued to enlighten me on the precarious situation of German Jewry, citing the deserted synagogues as proof. Only one shul in Munich functioned regularly, with its congregation numbering a scant fifty members on Shabbos. Its main entrance was always securely bolted and the elderly congregants were forced to use the back entrance. An armed attendant was stationed smartly at the door to ensure that all attendees were genuinely Jewish.

Forty years had already joined the annals of history since Hitler had embarked on his senseless rampage, yet the few remaining religious Jews still cowered fearfully in their vulnerable homes. The threat of a repeat performance haunted them on a daily basis, injecting their lives with fear and insecurity.

A young man from Konstat, a small village near the Swiss border, elucidated the dreadful circumstances with a fiery passion borne of despair. Prior to World War II, the Jewish population had numbered several thousand souls. In 1981, Konstat's Jewish community consisted of only one hundred and twenty people who harbored no hopes for future growth. The last Bar Mitzvah celebrated in the small village had taken place five years previous, for the younger generation had departed in search of friendlier shores. Elderly men trickled into Konstat to rest their weary bones and to collect their pensions.

Jewish life and vitality had basically evaporated in Germany's sordid environment, transforming the proud country into a large, Jewish cemetery. Assimilated Jews haughtily climbed the echelons of upper society while their abandoned souls languished under invisible tombstones. My belief that Hitler and his cohorts had been successfully eradicated from the face of the earth was suddenly shattered. The long tentacles of the Nazi movement still reached out to strangle the pitiful remnants of German Jewry.

Neo-Nazism was kicking up a storm in the civilized country, while the political leanings simply accentuated their nefarious desires. Germany was firmly opposed to the development of an independent Jewish state, and they utilized every opportunity to publicize their opinions. Their warped political policy seemed to have one goal in mind, namely, to damage the Jewish state as much as possible. Is it any wonder that my feelings for the advanced Aryan nation vacillated between disgust and revulsion?

The Torah Convocation successfully wound to a close, leaving everlasting impressions on all who were involved. At the conclusion of the inspiring week, printed reports of the conference were distributed to all attendees. One member eloquently expressed her thoughts concerning the lectures and presentations she had been privileged to observe and absorb.

"At 8:00 P.M. we met Rabbi Abraham Hecht, guest speaker from New York," she wrote. "He is most impressive and, though we were tired after such a long day, his talk on 'Israel Among the Nations' was so enthralling that we all listened attentively. Not that I agreed with all that he said, but his clarity and numerous stories told with a Sephardic flavor – he has the largest Sephardic Congregation back in Brooklyn, though he is not Sephardic – simply enthralled me!

"I literally swallowed Rabbi Hecht's words as he addressed us again, this time sharing with us his feelings about being in this blood-soaked country and the retreat area where the Nazi monsters had roamed. Due to the approach of Shavuos, Rabbi Hecht then spoke of a couple of the Ten Commandments (they were given on that holiday), about the Jewish people's survival and responsibilities. Again his words deeply affected me. His smile, humor and stories about his large congregation made up for what seemed to be at times indirect though interesting answers. Apparently, others enjoyed it as much.

"Friday night I dreamed that thousands of Jews were marching with me behind Rabbi Hecht, who came over to me and said, 'Look forward and behind and see how many strong we are!'

"I could not see the end of the crowd who were singing patriotic and freedom songs very loudly. I awoke with a start and decided not to take a trip on Shabbos."

The sentiments expressed by this member of the group mirrored the reactions of many. I was pleased to note that my trip to the basin of human atrocity had produced such positive results despite the discomfort involved. Encased in the glow of shared inspiration, I boarded the airplane heading towards the safe environs of New York. The experience had reinforced my understanding of the destruction of European Jewry, but I was more than glad to ponder my thoughts on comfortable and established ground.

After arriving home, I penned several letters to General E. C. Meyer, the Chief of Staff of the United States Army, to the Secretary of Defense, the Chief of Chaplains, and to the Chief of Naval Operations. I expressed my opinion that improvement of the conditions of Army personnel in Germany would undoubtedly engender improved morale.

General E. C. Meyers replied swiftly, as did many of the other officials I had addressed.

"Thank you for your letter of June 5th, 1981 in which you express your conviction that improvements to facilities and housing would contribute greatly to raising the morale of Army personnel in Germany," he wrote. "Provision of adequate living and working conditions is and will continue to be high on the army list of peace-time requirements."

The months following my return from Germany proved once again that time is the most remarkable antidote for traumatic experiences and disturbing memories. I slowly settled into blessed routine, but the difficult lessons I had learned in that infamous country continuously urged me to publicize what I had witnessed. The Holocaust venom was still poisoning German blood, placing our vulnerable brethren in a precarious position.

Senate

MONDAY, APRIL 25, 1966

The Senate met at 12 o'clock meridian, and was called to order by Hon. ROBERT C. BYRD, a Senator from the State of West Virginia.

Rabbi Dr. Abraham Hecht, president, Rabbinical Alliance of America, Brooklyn, N.Y., offered the following prayer:

אבינו שבשמים מלך העולם

Sovereign of the universe, Almighty G-d in Heaven, may this hour be an hour of favor and acceptance in Your sight.

Our hearts are lifted unto You in gratitude for Your mercies and kindness toward the people of these blessed United States. More especially, do we thank You, O L-rd, for bestowing upon this great land, legislators and statesmen who will guide with the help of Almighty, the destiny, and stir the hearts of men and women, young and old, to serve their country in truth and loyalty.

Bless this august assembly and their families. May they be granted peace of mind, serenity and spirit, and inner tranquility predicated upon faith and trust in G-d. May these who occupy themselves with the affairs of our country always faithfully seek Your guidance in pursuing its welfare, its advancement, its growth and security.

Pour down Your bountiful blessings upon our distinguished and beloved President, Lyndon B. Johnson, his family, and all the peoples of this great democracy, so that peace and prosperity, freedom and tolerance increase and endure throughout the length and breadth of its borders.

May we realize in our day the prophetic vision of Isaiah—LVIII—as engendered by the various programs advanced by this illustrious legislative body for the welfare of mankind.

To loose the fetters of wickedness,
To undo the bands of the yoke,
And to let the oppressed go free,
And that you break every yoke?
Is it not to deal your bread to the hungry,
And that you bring the poor that are cast out to thy house?
When thou seest the naked, that thou cover him,
And that thou hide not thyself from thine own flesh?

We pray to the Ruler of the universe that His blessing continue to be bestowed on all inhabitants of our country, that fears and dangers, prejudice and malice be removed from its borders, and that all its citizens regardless of race, color, or creed will know the joys of prosperity, tranquillity, and peace. Amen.

No. 68——9

DESIGNATION OF ACTING PRESIDENT PRO TEMPORE

The legislative clerk read the following letter:

U.S. SENATE,
PRESIDENT PRO TEMPORE,
Washington, D.C., April 25, 1966.
To the Senate:

Being temporarily absent from the Senate, I appoint Hon. ROBERT C. BYRD, a Senator from the State of West Virginia, to perform the duties of the Chair during my absence.
CARL HAYDEN,
President pro tempore.

Mr. BYRD of West Virginia thereupon took the chair as Acting President pro tempore.

THE JOURNAL

On request of Mr. MANSFIELD, and by unanimous consent, the reading of the Journal of the proceedings of Thursday, April 21, 1966, was dispensed with.

MESSAGES FROM THE PRESIDENT

Messages in writing from the President of the United States were communicated to the Senate by Mr. Jones, one of his secretaries.

REORGANIZATION PLAN NO. 3 OF 1966—MESSAGE FROM THE PRESIDENT (H. DOC. NO. 428)

The ACTING PRESIDENT pro tempore laid before the Senate the following message from the President of the United States, which was referred to the Committee on Government Operations:

To the Congress of the United States:

I transmit herewith Reorganization Plan No. 3 of 1966, prepared in accordance with the Reorganization Act of 1949, as amended, and providing for reorganization of health functions of the Department of Health, Education, and Welfare.

I

Today we face new challenges and unparalleled opportunities in the field of health. Building on the progress of the past several years, we have truly begun to match the achievements of our medicine to the needs of our people.

The task ahead is immense. As a nation, we will unceasingly pursue our research and learning, our training and building, our testing and treatment. But now our concern must also turn to the organization of our Federal health programs.

As citizens we are entitled to the very best health services our resources can provide.

As taxpayers, we demand the most efficient and economic health organizations that can be devised.

I ask the Congress to approve a reorganization plan to bring new strength to the administration of Federal health programs.

I propose a series of changes in the organization of the Public Health Service that will bring to all Americans a structure modern in design, more efficient in operation and better prepared to meet the great and growing needs of the future. Through such improvements we can achieve the full promise of the landmark health legislation enacted by the 89th Congress.

I do not propose these changes lightly. They follow a period of careful deliberation. For many months the Secretary of Health, Education, and Welfare and the Surgeon General have consulted leading experts in the Nation—physicians, administrators, scientists, and public health specialists. They have confirmed my belief that modernization and reorganization of the Public Health Service are urgently required and long overdue.

II

The Public Health Service is an operating agency of the Department of Health, Education, and Welfare. It is the principal arm of the Federal Government in the field of health. Its programs are among those most vital to our well-being.

Since 1953 more than 50 new programs have been placed in the Public Health Service. Its budget over the past 12 years has increased tenfold—from $250 million to $2.4 billion.

Today the organization of the Public Health Service is clearly obsolete. The requirement that new and expanding programs be administered through an organizational structure established by law more than two decades ago stands as a major obstacle to the fulfillment of our Nation's health goals.

As presently constituted, the Public Health Service is composed of four major components: National Institutes of Health, Bureau of State Services, Bureau of Medical Services, Office of the Surgeon General. Under present law, Public Health Service functions must be assigned only to these four components.

This structure was designed to provide separate administrative arrangements for health research, programs of State and local aid, health services, and executive staff resources. At a time when these functions could be neatly compartmentalized, the structure was adequate. But today the situation is different.

8441

Under recent legislation many new programs provide for an integrated attack on specific disease problems or health hazards in the environment by combining health services, State and local aid, and research. Each new program of this type necessarily is assigned to one of the three operating components of the Public Health Service. Yet none of these components is intended to administer programs involving such a variety of approaches.

Our health problems are difficult enough without having them complicated by outmoded organizational arrangements.

But if we merely take the step of integrating the four agencies within the Public Health Service we will not go far enough. More is required.

III

The Department of Health, Education, and Welfare performs major health or health-related functions which are not carried out through the Public Health Service, although they are closely related to its functions. Among these are health insurance for the aged, administered through the Social Security Administration; medical assistance for the needy, administered through the Welfare Administration; regulation of the manufacture, labeling, and distribution of drugs, carried out through the Food and Drug Administration; and grants-in-aid to States for vocational rehabilitation of the handicapped, administered by the Vocational Rehabilitation Administration.

Expenditures for health and health-related programs of the Department administered outside the Public Health Service have increased from $44 million in 1953 to an estimated $5.4 billion in 1967.

As the head of the Department, the Secretary of Health, Education, and Welfare is responsible for the administration and coordination of all the Department's health functions. He has clear authority over the programs I have just mentioned.

But today he lacks this essential authority over the Public Health Service. The functions of that agency are vested in the Surgeon General and not in the Secretary.

This diffusion of responsibility is unsound and unwise.

To secure the highest possible level of health services for the American people the Secretary of Health, Education, and Welfare must be given the authority to establish—and modify as necessary—the organizational structure for Public Health Service programs.

He must also have the authority to coordinate health functions throughout the Department. The reorganization plan I propose will accomplish these purposes. It will provide the Secretary with the flexibility to create new and responsive organizational arrangements to keep pace with the changing and dynamic nature of our health programs.

My views in this respect follow a basic principle of good government set by the Hoover Commission in 1949 when it recommended "that the department head should be given authority to determine the organization within his department."

IV

In summary, the reorganization plan would—

Transfer to the Secretary of Health, Education, and Welfare the functions now vested in the Surgeon General of the Public Health Service and in its various subordinate units—this transfer will not affect certain statutory advisory bodies such as the National Advisory Cancer and Heart Councils;

Abolish the four principal statutory components of the Public Health Service, including the offices held by their heads—the Bureau of Medical Services, the Bureau of State Services, the National Institutes of Health exclusive of its several research institutions such as the National Cancer and Heart Institutes, and the Office of the Surgeon General;

Authorize the Secretary to assign the functions transferred to him by the plan to officials and entities of the Public Health Service and to other agencies of the Department as he deems appropriate;

Thus, the Secretary would be enabled to assure that all health functions of the Department are carried out as effectively and economically as possible; given authority commensurate with his responsibility; and made responsible in fact for matters for which he is now, in any case, held accountable by the President, the Congress, and the people.

V

I have found, after investigation, that each reorganization included in the accompanying reorganization plan is necessary to accomplish one or more of the purposes set forth in section 2(a) of the Reorganization Act of 1949, as amended.

Should the reorganizations in the accompanying reorganization plan take effect, they will make possible more effective and efficient administration of the affected health programs. It is, however, not practicable at this time to itemize the reductions in expenditures which may result.

I strongly recommend that the Congress allow the reorganization plan to become effective.

LYNDON B. JOHNSON.

THE WHITE HOUSE, *April 25, 1966.*

WAIVER OF CALL OF THE CALENDAR

Mr. MANSFIELD. Mr. President, under rule VIII, I ask unanimous consent to waive the call of the calendar of measures that are not objected to.

The ACTING PRESIDENT pro tempore. Without objection, it is so ordered.

LIMITATION ON STATEMENTS DURING TRANSACTION OF ROUTINE MORNING BUSINESS

On request of Mr. MANSFIELD, and by unanimous consent, statements during the transaction of routine morning business were ordered limited to 3 minutes.

COMMITTEE MEETING DURING SENATE SESSION

Mr. ELLENDER. Mr. President, I ask unanimous consent that the Committee on Post Office and Civil Service be permitted to meet during the session of the Senate today.

The ACTING PRESIDENT pro tempore. Without objection, it is so ordered.

EXECUTIVE SESSION

Mr. MANSFIELD. Mr. President, I ask unanimous consent that the Senate proceed to consider executive business, for action on nominations.

The ACTING PRESIDENT pro tempore. Is there objection to the request of the Senator from Montana?

There being no objection, the Senate proceeded to the consideration of executive business.

EXECUTIVE MESSAGES REFERRED

The ACTING PRESIDENT pro tempore laid before the Senate messages from the President of the United States submitting sundry nominations, which were referred to the appropriate committees.

(For nominations this day received, see the end of Senate proceedings.)

The ACTING PRESIDENT pro tempore. If there be no reports of committees, the clerk will state the nominations on the Executive Calendar.

ENVIRONMENTAL SCIENCE SERVICES ADMINISTRATION

The Chief Clerk proceeded to read sundry nominations in the Environmental Science Services Administration.

Mr. MANSFIELD. Mr. President, I ask unanimous consent that the nominations be considered en bloc.

The ACTING PRESIDENT pro tempore. Without objection, the nominations are considered and confirmed en bloc.

Mr. MANSFIELD. Mr. President, I ask that the President be immediately notified of the confirmation of these nominations.

The ACTING PRESIDENT pro tempore. Without objection, the President will be notified forthwith.

LEGISLATIVE SESSION

On request of Mr. MANSFIELD, and by unanimous consent, the Senate resumed the consideration of legislative business.

THE CALENDAR

Mr. MANSFIELD. Mr. President, I ask unanimous consent that the Senate proceed to the consideration of Calendar Nos. 1099 and 1100.

The ACTING PRESIDENT pro tempore. Without objection, it is so ordered.

DISPOSAL OF MOLYBDENUM FROM THE NATIONAL STOCKPILE

The bill (H.R. 13369) to authorize the disposal of molybdenum from the national stockpile was considered, ordered to a third reading, read the third time, and passed.

Mr. MANSFIELD. Mr. President, I ask unanimous consent to have printed

Congressional Record

United States
of America
    PROCEEDINGS AND DEBATES OF THE 90th CONGRESS, SECOND SESSION

Vol. 114   **WASHINGTON, MONDAY, JULY 29, 1968**   *No. 133*

House of Representatives

The House met at 12 o'clock noon.
Rabbi Dr. Abraham B. Hecht, Shaare Zion Congregation, Brooklyn, N.Y., offered the following prayer:

אביע שבשפים - מלך השלם!

A-mighty G-d, ruler of the universe, we express our deep gratitude to you, for the miracle of civilization, we call America. The ideals of liberty, equality, and personal freedom bedrocks of our society, serve today to millions throughout the world, as the most desirable virtues of government.

We thank you, O' L-rd, for this august legislative body which constitutes the finest minds and sincerest hearts, illustrious and dedicated Representatives of all the people of our great Republic.

We pray that You will guide and direct these Members of Congress, to legislate fearlessly in the spirit of truth and justice; to remove the scourges of crime and violence threatening to destroy the fabric of our national security; to pursue the goals of universal peace with honor; to effectuate a conciliation between East and West; to assist the needy and the oppressed at home and abroad; and to recognize the valid claims of the Jewish State for support—moral and material.

We invoke the blessings of our Father in heaven upon every Member of Congress and upon their families. May the L-rd grant them good health, prosperity, and success in their endeavors for humanity.

We pray for the welfare of our Government, led by our distinguished President, Lyndon B. Johnson. May the policies of the Congress continue to be motivated by concern for the commonweal, steadied by moral compunctions, and sustained by moral courage.

In the words of the Psalmist—Psalm CXXXIV—we pray, "May the L-rd who made heaven and earth, bless you from Zion." Amen.

THE JOURNAL

The Journal of the proceedings of Friday, July 26, 1968, was read and approved.

MESSAGE FROM THE SENATE

A message from the Senate by Mr. Arrington, one of its clerks, announced

that the Senate had passed without amendment bills and a concurrent resolution of the House of the following titles:

H.R. 1648. An act for the relief of Martina Zubiri Garcia;
H.R. 2281. An act for the relief of Dwayne C. Cox and William D. Martin;
H.R. 6195. An act for the relief of Peter Balinas and Lee Balinas;
H.R. 6655. An act for the relief of Mary Jane Orloski;
H.R. 8391. An act for the relief of Adel Lessert Bellmard, Clement Lessert, Johephine Gonvil Pappan, Julie Gonvil Pappan, Pelagie Gonvil Francoeur de Aubri, Victore Gonvil Pappan, Marie Gonvil, Lafleche Gonvil, Louis Laventure, Elizabeth Carbonau Vertifelle, Pierce Carbonau, Louis Joncas, Basil Joncas, James Joncas, Elizabeth Datcherute, Joseph Butler, William Rodger, Joseph Cote, four children of Cicili Compare and Joseph James, or the heirs of any who may be deceased;
H.R. 9391. An act to amend section 376(a) of title 28, United States Code;
H.R. 10321. An act for the relief of Mrs. Claudette C. Donahue;
H.R. 10327. An act for the relief of Louis J. Falardeau, Irva G. Franger, Betty Klemcke, Wineta L. Welburn, and Emma L. McNeil, all individuals employed by the Department of the Army at Fort Sam Houston, Tex.;
H.R. 11381. An act for the relief of E. L. Townley, Otis T. Hawkins, and Leo T. Matous;
H.R. 12119. An act for the relief of Joseph M. Hepworth;
H.R. 14167. An act for the relief of Lydia M. Parsley;
H.R. 15864. An act to provide for the operation of the William Langer Jewel Bearing Plant at Rolla, N. Dak., and for other purposes; and
H. Con. Res. 798. Concurrent resolution authorizing the Clerk of the House of Representatives to make a change in the enrollment of H.R. 9098.

The message also announced that the Senate receded from its amendments to a bill of the House (H.R. 9098) entitled "An act to revise the boundaries of the Badlands National Monument in the State of South Dakota, to authorize exchanges of land mutually beneficial to the Oglala Sioux Tribe and the United States, and for other purposes."

The message also announced that the Senate had passed with amendments in which concurrence of the House is requested, bills of the House of the following titles:

H.R. 15758. An act to amend the Public Health Service Act so as to extend and improve the provisions relating to regional medical programs, to extend the authorization of grants for health of migratory agricultural workers, to provide for specialized facilities for alcoholics and narcotic addicts, and for other purposes; and
H.R. 16361. An act to provide additional revenue for the District of Columbia, and for other purposes.

The message also announced that the Senate insists upon its amendments to the bill (H.R. 16361) entitled "An act to provide additional revenue for the District of Columbia, and for other purposes," requests a conference with the House on the disagreeing votes of the two Houses thereon, and appoints Mr. Spong, Mr. Morse, and Mr. Morton to be the conferees on the part of the Senate.

The message also announced that the Senate disagrees to the amendments of the House to the bill (S. 3769) entitled "An act to amend the Higher Education Act of 1965, the National Defense Education Act of 1958, the National Vocational Student Loan Insurance Act of 1965, the Higher Education Facilities Act of 1963, and related acts," agree to the conference asked by the House on the disagreeing votes of the two Houses thereon, and appoints Mr. Morse, Mr. Yarborough, Mr. Clark, Mr. Randolph, Mr. Williams of New Jersey, Mr. Nelson, Mr. Prouty, Mr. Javits, Mr. Dominick, and Mr. Murphy to be the conferees on the part of the Senate.

The message also announced that the Senate had passed bills and a concurrent resolution of the following titles, in which the concurrence of the House is requested:

S. 908. An act for the relief of William D. Pender;
S. 3269. An act to consent to the New Hampshire-Vermont Interstate School Compact;
S. 3640. An act to establish a commission to study the organization, operation, and management of the executive branch of the Government, and to recommend changes necessary or desirable in the interest of governmental efficiency and economy;
S. 3724. An act to amend the Investment Company Act of 1940 and the Investment Advisers Act of 1940 to define the equitable standards governing relationships between investment companies and their investment

Down Under

I was privileged to visit numerous countries and regions while servicing the Sephardic community and manning my post on the Igud HaRabbanim. Meetings were held in the most far-flung corners of the globe, yet one journey in particular grabs first place for its foreign flavor. In the summer of 1976, I traveled to Australia, the continent that has earned the dubious distinction of being located somewhere "down under".

My grandson's Bar Mitzvah celebration was scheduled for mid-August in Melbourne, Australia. Overwhelmed with excitement and anticipation, my wife and I relaxed comfortably in our seats as the technological eagle winged its way toward our destination. It wasn't every day that a born and bred American citizen found himself traveling halfway across the globe for a family simcha. En-route to the distant land, I resolved to utilize every moment of my planned stay to the fullest. Upon my return to New York, I wanted to be the proud owner of several worthwhile Australian weeks.

Our airplane landed smoothly and efficiently, as did our assorted pieces of luggage. Buoyed by the interesting sights and unfamiliar surroundings, we felt ready to traverse the great Australian expanse without further ado. Walking along the paved streets of Melbourne, I surreptitiously glanced into deserted alleyways in search of a stray kangaroo. My disappointment upon recognizing the regular urban sights, sounds, and

pollution did not impinge on my boundless curiosity of the foreign land.

After setting down our belongings and getting reacquainted
with our Australian grandchildren, I was ready to explore the
Jewish communities located in this part of the Southern Hemisphere. Thinking about their interesting climate and seasons, I
couldn't help wondering how they managed to infuse the holidays with the proper atmosphere. After all, lighting the Chanukah menorah without a cold, snowy backdrop seemed nearly impossible. The same incongruence exists with a wintry Shavuos
and a warm Sukkos.

"Your grandchildren probably entertain the same thoughts
concerning Yomim Tovim in distant New York," I reminded myself wryly. "They cannot imagine celebrating Chanukah, Shavuos
or Sukkos under different circumstances."

These musings left me with a better understanding of why
two people can argue heatedly for hours on end, without reaching an agreement. Someone born in Australia can never fully
comprehend the mentality of an American and vice-versa. A person brought up with a distinct set of values and principles will
find it difficult to understand any differing opinions. Effort has to
be invested to picture oneself on the other side of the tennis
net, playing with the opponent's tools.

Placing my ruminations aside for future introspection, I proceeded to forge ties with the Sephardic communities in Australia. In New South Wales, I was pleased to discover that the Sephardim had established a strong, flourishing kehillah with all
necessary institutions and regulations. I gladly agreed to lecture
at various meetings and organizations in New South Wales, on a
variety of topics that interested the Australians of Sephardic descent. The congregation appreciated the detailed first-hand ac-
counts about their brethren in New York, and the information
about the Jews still residing in Arab countries.

Rabbi Simon Silas, the Chief Rabbi of the Sephardic community in New South Wales, expressed his appreciation for the American view I had discussed and explained.

"On behalf of my congregation and myself, I wish to thank you most sincerely for the stimulating and in-depth report you gave us on the Jews in Arab lands as well as Sephardic life in New York City," he wrote, a short while after my visit.

The Sephardic community of Victoria also received me graciously, and there, too, I delivered several lectures to varied crowds. It was interesting to note how the local newspapers chose to describe my visit and which experiences they highlighted in their reports.

One of the daily newspapers in Melbourne used my visit as the headlines in the Friday edition, on August 27th.

"Ashkenazi Rabbi with Influence – Even with Sephardim", the headlines proclaimed.

"A rabbi who has worked with Kurt Waldheim (United Nations Secretary General), is friends with the U.S. Ambassador to Syria…is somewhat of a phenomenon.

"Indeed, Rabbi Dr. Abraham Hecht, one of the leading rabbis of the U.S., and President of the Rabbinical Alliance of the U.S. and Canada, is a humanitarian as well as a scholar and spiritual leader; in short – a mentsch."

The journalist then discussed my interesting position as the leader of the Sephardic community. The passage of time had not dulled the glaring contradiction and my background still served to pique the curiosity of the Sephardim.

"Though himself an Ashkenazi, he is rabbi of the largest Sephardic Association in America – a community of 30,000 Jews…"

An enterprising journalist of a different newspaper found my American descent interesting enough to research and subsequently describe in detail to the Australian public.

"An Ashkenazi rabbi heading the biggest Sephardic centre in

the Western Hemisphere, Rabbi Hecht is a fourth generation American – a real "Yankee Doodle", he says.

"He was born in Brooklyn in 1922, descendant of a Galician family who went to the United States in 1890. His parents had six sons. All of them became rabbis, with almost every major Jewish urban centre throughout the United States having been served at one time or another by at least one of the Hecht brothers…

"Rabbi Hecht is greatly impressed with Sydney, but warns the community that it will face strong assimilation unless the children will be given a good, solid Jewish education…

"…'When Jewish communities the world over realize that there is a strong contingent "down-under" beating the same drums, it will give every Jew the world-over further encouragement,' Rabbi Hecht says."

Aside from the lectures I gave to the Sephardic communities in Victoria and New South Wales, I also contacted the Lubavitcher community in Melbourne. I spoke to the community at large in the home of Mr. and Mrs. Sam Feiglin for the benefit of Yeshivas Beth Rivkah, the Lubavitcher girls' school. Despite my strong affiliation and connections with the Sephardim, I still very much identified with Chassidus which had shown me the proper way of life in the American wastelands. My situation might have appeared interesting and bizarre, yet I found the description of a Lubavitcher Sephardic Rabbi quite comfortable.

The days and weeks passed quickly, without allowing me any time to breathe or relax. I enjoyed the constant hustle and bustle of attending meetings, discussions and lectures in an unfamiliar land. My daughter's lively family spiced the visit with feelings of home, while the strange surroundings continuously reminded me that Australia really is situated halfway around the globe.

The hands of time seemed to rush forward without considering the ramifications of its speedy passage. Once again, my wife and I found ourselves at the airport preparing for a lengthy journey. While lugging our oversized baggage, we parted with our young Australian family, wondering when we would see each other again. Our wishes for the young Bar Mitzvah boy floated lazily in the relaxed Australian atmosphere as our airplane started nosing its way between the clouds.

The endless hours of travel provided me with ample time to absorb my experiences and readjust to blessed routine. I was returning to New York with several suitcases, a few pieces of hand luggage and a virtual treasure trove of experiences.

H 7710   CONGRESSIONAL RECORD — HOUSE   *July 29, 1968*

advisers and principal underwriters, and for other purposes; and

S. Con. Res. 78. Concurrent resolution favoring the suspension of deportation of certain aliens.

RABBI DR. ABRAHAM B. HECHT

(Mr. PODELL asked and was given permission to address the House for 1 minute, and to revise and extend his remarks.)

Mr. PODELL. Mr. Speaker, we were privileged, and the Congress was truly honored this morning to welcome Rabbi Abraham B. Hecht, who is the spiritual leader of the Temple Shaare Zion of Brooklyn, N.Y.—a temple which is the symbol of the Sephardic community of Brooklyn, N.Y., today.

Rabbi Abraham Hecht is one of six brothers, all of whom are rabbis. He is a noted scholar, a leading teacher, a great humanitarian, and a great educator. Our House of Representatives was truly honored on this occasion.

Mr. Speaker, I believe the best way to express the spirit of Rabbi Hecht is to quote from the Torah itself:

לא בחיל, לא בכח, כי אם ברוחי

Which means "not with thy strength, not with thy sword, but only with My spirit, saith the L—rd."

And thus Rabbi Hecht is bringing to his community the great spirit of the Lord in the hearts of all mankind. The world at war could well take heed of the spirit of Rabbi Abraham Hecht.

WHAT'S RIGHT WITH AMERICA

(Mr. ICHORD asked and was given permission to address the House for 1 minute and to revise and extend his remarks.)

Mr. ICHORD. Mr. Speaker, Thomas Jefferson once wrote:

Laws and institutions must go hand in hand with the progress of the human mind. As that becomes more developed, more enlightened, as new discoveries are made, new truths disclosed, and manners and opinions change with the change of circumstances, institutions must advance also, and keep pace with the times.

Most of us recognize the necessity of change to keep pace with the times. But we cannot have change merely for the sake of change at the sacrifice of basic principles which have made this country great.

Dr. Solomon Garb, of the University of Missouri, an outstanding American of great intellect and discerning mind, has written a new book to be published in the near future entitled "What's Right With America," rather than was is wrong.

I would recommend this book for the reading of all legislators and governmental officials. I ask unanimous consent to have printed in the Extensions of Remarks of the RECORD, the introduction of his book "What's Right With America," as well as excerpts from the book concerning the pitfalls of the proposed negative income tax or guaranteed income. America should beware of this deadly trap.

The SPEAKER. Without objection, it is so ordered.

There was no objection.

LEGISLATIVE PROGRAM

(Mr. ALBERT asked and was given permission to address the House for 1 minute and to revise and extend his remarks.)

Mr. ALBERT. Mr. Speaker, I take this time to alert the House that later in the day the distinguished chairman of the Committee on Post Office and Civil Service will, by unanimous consent, seek to take from the Speaker's table and bring before the House H.R. 15387, to amend title 39, United States Code, to provide for disciplinary action against employees in the postal field service who assault other employees in such service in the performance of official duties, and for other purposes, with Senate amendments thereto, disagree with the Senate amendments, and ask for a conference with the Senate. The gentleman from New York [Mr. DULSKI] has advised me that he will make that unanimous-consent request at some later time today.

(Mr. SIKES asked and was given permission to address the House for 1 minute and to revise and extend his remarks.)

[Mr. SIKES addressed the House. His remarks will appear hereafter in the Extensions of Remarks.]

CORRECTION OF ROLLCALL

Mr. CEDERBERG. Mr. Speaker, on rollcall No. 286, appearing in the RECORD for Friday, July 26, 1968, on page H7658, I am listed as having been present for a quorum call. As it was necessary for me to be in my district that day, I was not present and did not answer to my name, and so I ask unanimous consent that the permanent RECORD and Journal be corrected accordingly.

The SPEAKER. Is there objection to the request of the gentleman from Michigan?

There was no objection.

MILITARY CONSTRUCTION APPROPRIATIONS, 1969

Mr. SIKES. Mr. Speaker, I move that the House resolve itself into the Committee of the Whole House on the State of the Union for the consideration of the bill (H.R. 18785) making appropriations for military construction for the Department of Defense for the fiscal year ending June 30, 1969, and for other purposes; and pending that motion, Mr. Speaker, I ask unanimous consent that general debate be limited to 1 hour, the time to be equally divided and controlled by the gentleman from Michigan [Mr. CEDERBERG] and myself.

The SPEAKER. Is there objection to the request of the gentleman from Florida?

There was no objection.

CALL OF THE HOUSE

Mr. PELLY. Mr. Speaker, I make the point of order that a quorum is not present.

The SPEAKER. Evidently a quorum is not present.

Mr. ALBERT. Mr. Speaker, I move a call of the House.

A call of the House was ordered.

The Clerk called the roll, and the following Members failed to answer to their names:

[Roll No. 290]

Adair	Esch	Lipscomb
Anderson, Tenn.	Evins, Tenn.	Long, La.
Ashley	Fino	Lukens
Blackburn	Flood	McCloskeyMcClure
Blanton	Fulton, Tenn.	McClure
Bolton	Gardner	Moorhead
Brock	Goodell	Morris, N. Mex.
Brown, Mich.	Gubser	Nelsen
Burke, Fla.	Hansen, Idaho	Quie
Burton, Utah	Hathaway	Rarick
Button	Hawkins	Resnick
Conte	Hébert	Rhodes, Ariz.
Conyers	Herlong	Satterfield
Cramer	Hohfield	Schweiker
Davis, Wis.	Holland	Steed
de la Garza	Howard	Taft
Diggs	Karsten	Thompson, Ga.
Dole	Kirwan	Waggoner
Edwards, Ala.	Kupferman	Wampler
	Kuykendall	
	Laird	

The SPEAKER. On this rollcall, 369 Members have answered to their names, a quorum.

By unanimous consent, further proceedings under the call were dispensed with.

MILITARY CONSTRUCTION APPROPRIATIONS, 1969

The SPEAKER. The question is on the motion offered by the gentleman from Florida [Mr. SIKES].

The motion was agreed to.

IN THE COMMITTEE OF THE WHOLE

Accordingly the House resolved itself into the Committee of the Whole House on the State of the Union for the consideration of the bill (H.R. 18785) making appropriations for military construction for the Department of Defense for the fiscal year ending June 30, 1969, and for other purposes, with Mr. ULLMAN in the chair.

The Clerk read the title of the bill.

By unanimous consent, the first reading of the bill was dispensed with.

The CHAIRMAN. The gentleman from Florida [Mr. SIKES] is recognized.

(Mr. SIKES asked and was given permission to revise and extend his remarks.)

Mr. SIKES. Mr. Chairman, H.R. 18785, making appropriations for military construction for the Department of Defense for fiscal 1969, is the most austere construction program in recent history. I am not happy that such is the case. There are too many military bases on which facilities are substandard and inadequate. This is particularly true of housing, and I refer both to family housing and to housing for officers and enlisted men. This subcommittee has had particular concern with the morale factors resulting from a lack of comfortable and satisfactory housing. We are certain this has an adverse effect on retention rates— a very important matter to the services, because retention insures readily available skills and avoids training costs.

By contrast, the House is awaiting action on one of the largest defense appropriation bills in history. Yet in that bill also, very severe cuts were made. Some were in nonessential areas. But additional serious cuts were necessitated by the mandatory budget reductions voted

Congressional Record

United States of America   PROCEEDINGS AND DEBATES OF THE 90th CONGRESS, SECOND SESSION

Vol. 114	WASHINGTON, MONDAY, JULY 29, 1968	No. 133

House of Representatives

The House met at 12 o'clock noon.

Rabbi Dr. Abraham B. Hecht, Shaare Zion Congregation, Brooklyn, N.Y., offered the following prayer:

אבינו שבשמים - מלך העולם!

A-mighty G-d, ruler of the universe, we express our deep gratitude to you, for the miracle of civilization, we call America. The ideals of liberty, equality, and personal freedom bedrocks of our society, serve today to millions throughout the world, as the most desirable virtues of government.

We thank you, O' L-rd, for this august legislative body which constitutes the finest minds and sincerest hearts, illustrious and dedicated Representatives of all the people of our great Republic.

We pray that You will guide and direct these Members of Congress, to legislate fearlessly in the spirit of truth and justice; to remove the scourges of crime and violence threatening to destroy the fabric of our national security; to pursue the goals of universal peace with honor; to effectuate a conciliation between East and West; to assist the needy and the oppressed at home and abroad; and to recognize the valid claims of the Jewish State for support—moral and material.

We invoke the blessings of our Father in heaven upon every Member of Congress and upon their families. May the L-rd grant them good health, prosperity, and success in their endeavors for humanity.

We pray for the welfare of our Government, led by our distinguished President, Lyndon B. Johnson. May the policies of the Congress continue to be motivated by concern for the commonweal, steadied by moral compunctions, and sustained by moral courage.

In the words of the Psalmist—Psalm CXXXIV—we pray, "May the L-rd who made heaven and earth, bless you from Zion." Amen.

THE JOURNAL

The Journal of the proceedings of Friday, July 26, 1968, was read and approved.

MESSAGE FROM THE SENATE

A message from the Senate by Mr. Arrington, one of its clerks, announced that the Senate had passed without amendment bills and a concurrent resolution of the House of the following titles:

H.R. 1648. An act for the relief of Martina Zubiri Garcia;

H.R. 2281. An act for the relief of Dwayne C. Cox and William D. Martin;

H.R. 6195. An act for the relief of Peter Balinas and Lee Balinas;

H.R. 6655. An act for the relief of Mary Jane Orloski;

H.R. 8391. An act for the relief of Adel Lessert Bellmard, Clement Lessert, Johephine Gonvil Pappan, Julie Gonvil Pappan, Pelagie Gonvil Franceour de Aubri, Victore Gonvil Pappan, Marie Gonvil, Lafleche Gonvil, Louis Laventure, Elizabeth Carbonau Vertifelle, Pierce Carbonau, Louis Joncas, Basil Joncas, James Joncas, Elizabeth Datcherute, Joseph Butler, William Rodger, Joseph Cote, four children of Cicili Compare and Joseph James, or the heirs of any who may be deceased;

H.R. 9391. An act to amend section 376(a) of title 28, United States Code;

H.R. 10321. An act for the relief of Mrs. Claudette C. Donahue;

H.R. 10327. An act for the relief of Louis J. Falardeau, Irva G. Franger, Betty Klemcke, Wineta L. Welburn, and Emma L. McNeil, all individuals employed by the Department of the Army at Fort Sam Houston, Tex.;

H.R. 11381. An act for the relief of E. L. Townley, Otis T. Hawkins, and Leo T. Matous;

H.R. 12119. An act for the relief of Joseph M. Hepworth;

H.R. 14167. An act for the relief of Lydia M. Parsley;

H.R. 15864. An act to provide for the operation of the William Langer Jewel Bearing Plant at Rolla, N. Dak., and for other purposes; and

H. Con. Res. 798. Concurrent resolution authorizing the Clerk of the House of Representatives to make a change in the enrollment of H.R. 9098.

The message also announced that the Senate receded from its amendments to a bill of the House (H.R. 9098) entitled "An act to revise the boundaries of the Badlands National Monument in the State of South Dakota, to authorize exchanges of land mutually beneficial to the Oglala Sioux Tribe and the United States, and for other purposes."

The message also announced that the Senate had passed with amendments in which concurrence of the House is requested, bills of the House of the following titles:

H.R. 15758. An act to amend the Public Health Service Act so as to extend and improve the provisions relating to regional medical programs, to extend the authorization of grants for health of migratory agricultural workers, to provide for specialized facilities for alcoholics and narcotic addicts, and for other purposes; and

H.R. 16361. An act to provide additional revenue for the District of Columbia, and for other purposes.

The message also announced that the Senate insists upon its amendments to the bill (H.R. 16361) entitled "An act to provide additional revenue for the District of Columbia, and for other purposes," requests a conference with the House on the disagreeing votes of the two Houses thereon, and appoints Mr. Spong, Mr. Morse, and Mr. Morton to be the conferees on the part of the Senate.

The message also announced that the Senate disagrees to the amendments of the House to the bill (S. 3769) entitled "An act to amend the Higher Education Act of 1965, the National Defense Education Act of 1958, the National Vocational Student Loan Insurance Act of 1965, the Higher Education Facilities Act of 1963, and related acts," agree to the conference asked by the House on the disagreeing votes of the two Houses thereon, and appoints Mr. Morse, Mr. Yarborough, Mr. Clark, Mr. Randolph, Mr. Williams of New Jersey, Mr. Nelson, Mr. Prouty, Mr. Javits, Mr. Dominick, and Mr. Murphy to be the conferees on the part of the Senate.

The message also announced that the Senate had passed bills and a concurrent resolution of the following titles, in which the concurrence of the House is requested:

S. 908. An act for the relief of William D. Pender;

S. 3269. An act to consent to the New Hampshire-Vermont Interstate School Compact;

S. 3640. An act to establish a commission to study the organization, operation, and management of the executive branch of the Government, and to recommend changes necessary or desirable in the interest of governmental efficiency and economy;

S. 3724. An act to amend the Investment Company Act of 1940 and the Investment Advisers Act of 1940 to define the equitable standards governing relationships between investment companies and their investment

H 7710 CONGRESSIONAL RECORD — HOUSE *July 29, 1968*

advisers and principal underwriters, and for other purposes; and

S. Con. Res. 78. Concurrent resolution favoring the suspension of deportation of certain aliens.

RABBI DR. ABRAHAM B. HECHT

(Mr. PODELL asked and was given permission to address the House for 1 minute, and to revise and extend his remarks.)

Mr. PODELL. Mr. Speaker, we were privileged, and the Congress was truly honored this morning to welcome Rabbi Abraham B. Hecht, who is the spiritual leader of the Temple Shaare Zion of Brooklyn, N.Y.—a temple which is the symbol of the Sephardic community of Brooklyn, N.Y., today.

Rabbi Abraham Hecht is one of six brothers, all of whom are rabbis. He is a noted scholar, a leading teacher, a great humanitarian, and a great educator. Our House of Representatives was truly honored on this occasion.

Mr. Speaker, I believe the best way to express the spirit of Rabbi Hecht is to quote from the Torah itself:

לא בחיל, לא בכוח, כי אם ברוחי

Which means "not with thy strength, not with thy sword, but only with My spirit, saith the L-rd."

And thus Rabbi Hecht is bringing to his community the great spirit of the Lord in the hearts of all mankind. The world at war could well take heed of the spirit of Rabbi Abraham Hecht.

WHAT'S RIGHT WITH AMERICA

(Mr. ICHORD asked and was given permission to address the House for 1 minute and to revise and extend his remarks.)

Mr. ICHORD. Mr. Speaker, Thomas Jefferson once wrote:

Laws and institutions must go hand in hand with the progress of the human mind. As that becomes more developed, more enlightened, as new discoveries are made, new truths disclosed, and manners and opinions change with the change of circumstances, institutions must advance also, and keep pace with the times.

Most of us recognize the necessity of change to keep pace with the times. But we cannot have change merely for the sake of change at the sacrifice of basic principles which have made this country great.

Dr. Solomon Garb, of the University of Missouri, an outstanding American of great intellect and discerning mind, has written a new book to be published in the near future entitled "What's Right With America," rather than was is wrong.

I would recommend this book for the reading of all legislators and governmental officials. I ask unanimous consent to have printed in the Extensions of Remarks of the RECORD, the introduction of his book "What's Right With America," as well as excerpts from the book concerning the pitfalls of the proposed negative income tax or guaranteed income. America should beware of this deadly trap.

The SPEAKER. Without objection, it is so ordered.

There was no objection.

LEGISLATIVE PROGRAM

(Mr. ALBERT asked and was given permission to address the House for 1 minute and to revise and extend his remarks.)

Mr ALBERT. Mr. Speaker, I take this time to alert the House that later in the day the distinguished chairman of the Committee on Post Office and Civil Service will, by unanimous consent, seek to take from the Speaker's table and bring before the House H.R. 15387, to amend title 39, United States Code, to provide for disciplinary action against employees in the postal field service who assault other employees in such service in the performance of official duties, and for other purposes, with Senate amendments thereto, disagree with the Senate amendments, and ask for a conference with the Senate. The gentleman from New York [Mr. DULSKI] has advised me that he will make that unanimous-consent request at some later time today.

(Mr. SIKES asked and was given permission to address the House for 1 minute and to revise and extend his remarks.)

[Mr. SIKES addressed the House. His remarks will appear hereafter in the Extensions of Remarks.]

CORRECTION OF ROLLCALL

Mr. CEDERBERG. Mr. Speaker, on rollcall No. 286, appearing in the RECORD for Friday, July 26, 1968, on page H7658, I am listed as having been present for a quorum call. As it was necessary for me to be in my district that day, I was not present and did not answer to my name, and so I ask unanimous consent that the permanent RECORD and Journal be corrected accordingly.

The SPEAKER. Is there objection to the request of the gentleman from Michigan?

There was no objection.

MILITARY CONSTRUCTION APPROPRIATIONS, 1969

Mr. SIKES. Mr. Speaker, I move that the House resolve itself into the Committee of the Whole House on the State of the Union for the consideration of the bill (H.R. 18785) making appropriations for military construction for the Department of Defense for the fiscal year ending June 30, 1969, and for other purposes; and pending that motion, Mr. Speaker, I ask unanimous consent that general debate be limited to 1 hour, the time to be equally divided and controlled by the gentleman from Michigan [Mr. CEDERBERG] and myself.

The SPEAKER. Is there objection to the request of the gentleman from Florida?

There was no objection.

CALL OF THE HOUSE

Mr. PELLY. Mr. Speaker, I make the point of order that a quorum is not present.

The SPEAKER. Evidently a quorum is not present.

Mr. ALBERT. Mr. Speaker, I move a call of the House.

A call of the House was ordered.

The Clerk called the roll, and the following Members failed to answer to their names:

[Roll No. 290]

Adair	Esch	Lipscomb
Anderson,	Evins, Tenn.	Long, La.
Tenn.	Fino	Lukens
Ashley	Flood	McCloskey
Blackburn	Fulton, Tenn.	McClure
Blanton	Gardner	Moorhead
Bolton	Goodell	Morris, N. Mex.
Brock	Gubser	Nelsen
Brown, Mich.	Hansen, Idaho	Quie
Burke, Fla.	Hathaway	Rarick
Burton, Utah	Hawkins	Resnick
Button	Hébert	Rhodes, Ariz.
Conte	Herlong	Satterfield
Conyers	Holifield	Schweiker
Corman	Holland	Steed
Cramer	Howard	Taft
Davis, Wis.	Karsten	Thompson, Ga.
de la Garza	Kirwan	Waggoner
Diggs	Kupferman	Wampler
Dole	Kuykendall	
Edwards, Ala.	Laird	

The SPEAKER. On this rollcall, 369 Members have answered to their names, a quorum.

By unanimous consent, further proceedings under the call were dispensed with.

MILITARY CONSTRUCTION APPROPRIATIONS, 1969

The SPEAKER. The question is on the motion offered by the gentleman from Florida [Mr. SIKES].

The motion was agreed to.

IN THE COMMITTEE OF THE WHOLE

Accordingly the House resolved itself into the Committee of the Whole House on the State of the Union for the consideration of the bill (H.R. 18785) making appropriations for military construction for the Department of Defense for the fiscal year ending June 30, 1969, and for other purposes, with Mr. ULLMAN in the chair.

The Clerk read the title of the bill.

By unanimous consent, the first reading of the bill was dispensed with.

The CHAIRMAN. The gentleman from Florida [Mr. SIKES] is recognized.

(Mr. SIKES asked and was given permission to revise and extend his remarks.)

Mr. SIKES. Mr. Chairman, H.R. 18785, making appropriations for military construction for the Department of Defense for fiscal 1969, is the most austere construction program in recent history. I am not happy that such is the case. There are too many military bases on which facilities are substandard and inadequate. This is particularly true of housing, and I refer both to family housing and to housing for officers and enlisted men. This subcommittee has had particular concern with the morale factors resulting from a lack of comfortable and satisfactory housing. We are certain this has an adverse effect on retention rates— a very important matter to the services, because retention insures readily available skills and avoids training costs.

By contrast, the House is awaiting action on one of the largest defense appropriation bills in history. Yet in that bill also, very severe cuts were made. Some were in nonessential areas. But additional serious cuts were necessitated by the mandatory budget reductions voted

"Who is a Jew?"

Throughout the tests and travails of life, there was always one guiding light that suffused my path with unquestionable clarity. I witnessed numerous upheavals and reforms as well as countless disasters and tragedies that could have felled the strongest oak in Yellowstone National Park. The redeeming vitamin that has strengthened the hearts of our ancestors during the darkest times of Jewish history continues to inject streams of courage in our faltering veins and wounded limbs. It is a renowned piece of information that keeps every Jew individually, and our nation as a whole, standing majestically amongst the scraggly bushes that comprise today's modern society.

"Am Yisroel Chai" – the Jewish nation has been promised eternal survival. The nations of the world can be compared to scattered sand dunes. At times, they might appear large and overbearing but their fickle strength quails at the slightest wind. Klal Yisroel, in contrast, is an unconquerable mountain, unfazed by situation and circumstance. Our rights are often trampled by nefarious climbers, yet our peak is always pointed upward, in purposeful pursuit.

Our continuity is the basis of our survival. Therefore, anything that threatens to disrupt the holy chain is cause for fear and suspicion. More than thirty years ago, a disturbing issue came to light in the world's pinnacle of kedushah. Eretz Yisroel was, and still is plagued with this virulent scam that has been aided and abetted by Israel's governing body.

On July 7, 1950 the governing body in Israel ratified the Law of Return, stating that "every Jew has the right to come to Israel as an immigrant". What the law failed to elucidate was what the precise qualifications that label a person Jewish are. Controversy raged for many long years until an ignominious decision was reached. Chok Hashvus, the ill-fated Law of Return, was amended on the 11th of Adar, to identify Jews as "one born to a Jewish mother, or one who has converted".

At first glance, the innocuous law appears harmless and understandable. Throughout history, the guidelines defining one's Jewish status included either the mother's proven Jewishness or a proper conversion. The Law of Return stipulates the same well-known, halachic qualifications, yet a minor omission renders the law completely unacceptable. Chok Hashvus does not obligate non-Jews to undergo a conversion "kehalacha", as Jewish law dictates. Thus, any unidentified hocus-pocus procedure that has been allowed to masquerade in Reform and Conservative circles as true conversion would now be deemed acceptable by the Land of Israel. Certificates attesting to an immigrant's Jewish status would be freely distributed to anyone claiming to have undergone some form of conversion. Eretz Yisroel, the holiest country worldwide, was destined to become a welcoming home for multitudes of insincere converts.

Jewish Orthodox communities in every corner of the global network vehemently protested the outrageous display of negligence. Well-founded fears and suspicions soon translated into unstinting action directed against the incongruities blatantly unveiled in the Law of Return. The disastrous ramifications of questionable conversions spurred a host of rallies, petitions and organizations with a singular goal in mind. One word, 'kehalacha', spelled the difference between reprieve and calamity, yet its inclusion in the Chok Hashvus seemed close to impossible.

The Lubavitcher Rebbe zt"l was greatly distressed by the unfolding events and utilized all of his connections to prevent disaster. He foresaw the far-reaching results of the alarming Knesset decision and wasted no time in publicizing his reservations. A Gentile walking through the hallowed streets of Yerushalayim, costumed in the typical Yerushalmi garb and speaking Hebrew fluently, still remains a non-Jew. The document certifying his alleged conversion at the behest of a Reform rabbi is not worth the paper it was written on. The purposeless charade is as ineffectual as a confused giraffe determinedly adopting the mannerisms and lifestyle of a furry white rabbit. Despite its best attempts to blend into its adopted family and the animals' assurances that he really is a rabbit, a giraffe will always remain a giraffe.

If the only damage done would have been isolated cases of mistaken identity, the situation would not have engendered such immediate and drastic actions. Unfortunately, the glaring facts provided timber for an uncontrollable conflagration that threatened the very essence of Klal Yisroel's continuity. Jews of questionable lineage were now allowed to populate the small country, without censure. One could not determine whether the new immigrants were actually Jewish, or Gentiles who had been subjected to a Reform rabbi's meaningless rituals to attain their worthless certificates. Intermarriage became a widespread problem due to the dubious authenticity of the dime-a-dozen conversions.

As the president of the Igud Harabbanim of America, I received countless reports from around the world concerning this inexcusable outrage. The Orthodox communities seethed with indignation at the poisoned spear ruthlessly piercing our very existence. Official declarations against the Law of Return were publicized to awaken the collective conscience of the Jewish nation.

Erev Rosh Chodesh Sivan, 5730 (June, 1970), Chief Rabbi Y. Nissim and Chief Rabbi I. Unterman of Eretz Yisroel expressed their unequivocal opinion concerning this painful issue. Following are several points that comprised their declaration.

Every conversion performed, both in Israel and outside of Israel, which is not in accordance with the Halacha which has been fixed and permanent from the giving of the Torah on Har Sinai until the present day, is an invalid conversion. A non-Jew can become a Jew only through conversion in accordance with the Halacha.

It is forbidden by the Torah for those in charge of the registration of citizens to register one who is not Jewish and has not yet converted according to the Halacha, as a Jew.

The Chief Rabbinate turns to the government with an urgent plea to present to the Knesset an amendment to the Law by the addition of the words "in accordance with the Halacha" (i.e. kehalacha).

If, Chas V'shalom, the above-mentioned law is not amended, it is the duty of the religious representatives to leave the government.

The psak din issued by the Chief Rabbinate of Israel mirrored the rulings of all Torah giants who delved into the issue. Various steps were taken to ensure that the law would be amended, but the process was not simple. The Lubavitcher Rebbe zt"l advised that telegrams and letters should be sent to Golda Meir, the Prime Minister of Israel, urging her to save the future of Klal Yisroel. Forms were sent out all over the world with suggested text drafts, urging everyone to take a stand in the "Mihu Yehudi" campaign.

Thousands of telegrams and letters poured into the offices of the governing body of Israel, proclaiming their important messages in staggering piles of petitions. American Jews felt duty-bound to voice their outrage in the Prime Minister's office through the medium of paper and pen. This telegram crusade continued for many long months, generating an overwhelming response from even the most distant, far-flung communities.

During the summer months of 1971, R' Moshe Feinstein zt"l, penned an urgent letter to the directors of all religious summer camps. He requested that Friday, the fifteenth day of Av, all campers and staff members should assemble in their respective locations approximately an hour after Shacharis. The Gaon chose several chapters of Tehillim, including the fifteen shir hamaalos, to be recited posuk by posuk. At the completion of the specified chapters, he recommended that forms for telegrams should be handed out and all attendees should affix their names and addresses to the forms. These telegrams, proclaiming the importance of retaining our nation's special status, would all be forwarded to the government in Israel.

The difficult issue was being met head-on with various strategies, for keeping quiet in the face of such a calamity was suicidal. As tension escalated in the explosive cauldron, I resolved to utilize my position for this worthy cause.

E 6470   **CONGRESSIONAL RECORD** — *Extensions of Remarks*   *December 5, 1975*

A TRIBUTE TO RABBI ABRAHAM B. HECHT

HON. STEPHEN J. SOLARZ
OF NEW YORK

IN THE HOUSE OF REPRESENTATIVES

Thursday, December 4, 1975

Mr. SOLARZ. Mr. Speaker, I rise today to pay tribute to a constituent and good friend, Rabbi Abraham B. Hecht.

As a devoted spiritual and civic leader of the Jewish community, Rabbi Hecht has worked tirelessly and with boundless energy on many worthy projects—most notably on the fight to secure emigration rights for Syrian Jews. Rabbi Hecht has exhibited noble leadership in his organizing endeavors tempered with a humanistic dedication to the cause of freeing Syrian Jews. I have been fortunate to be able to join with Rabbi Hecht in this important cause and his inspirational dedication has served as a model of courage and humanity in seeking the inalienable human rights of freedom and security for this group of Jews in search of their homeland.

I am privileged to represent the largest Sephardic Jewish community in the world, outside of the Middle East, and certainly, this community is in good hands under the talented and committed leadership of Rabbi Hecht. In Hebrew the word rabbi means "teacher" and few are more deserving of this title than Rabbi Hecht. In setting up educational centers, classes, lecture series, and numerous scholarly endeavors, he has demonstrated his ability to organize and implement educational programs of the highest calibre.

Mr. Speaker, at this time I would like to insert into the RECORD an article that appeared in the Jewish Press about Rabbi Abraham B. Hecht—a dedicated and inspirational leader of the Jewish community.

[From the Jewish Press, November 28, 1975]

RABBI DR. ABRAHAM B. HECHT

(By Chaim Yerushalmi)

The Sephardim are known to be a very close-knit people. Years of difficulty with the Ashkenazim have made them understandably clannish and a bit chauvinistic about their particular status and ancestry. Though today, the traditional rivalry and enmity between chassidim and misnagdim has broken down almost completely, and a marriage between the two is no longer rare, the barriers between the Sephardim and Ashkenazim are still unfortunately very much in evidence.

As marriage between the two groups, which would go a long way towards integrating them, is still not common place, it is especially surprising that for their most important religious activities, involving a spiritual leader, the Sephardim of Flatbush have chosen an Ashkenazic rabbi.

And these Sephardim are not just a small, isolated group. They constitute the largest Syrian Jewish community outside of the Middle East. Their Shaare Zion Congregation is one of the biggest Sephardic centers in the Western Hemisphere. They have created an entire community of schools, kosher stores and businesses along the southern part of Ocean Parkway in Brooklyn.

It is thus a particular tribute to Rabbi Dr. Abraham B. Hecht that he was selected almost two decades ago to officiate at Shaare Zion, and it is a further testimonial to him that he has maintained his durability there.

Rabbi Hecht is not only an Ashkenazi, but he is also a Lubavitcher chassid and a fourth generation American.

He was born in Brooklyn in 1922 and his father, Samuel, (also a native American) was descended from an old Galician family, who came here in 1890. His mother, Sadie, also hailed from Galicia. Incidentally, the senior Hechts produced six sons who are rabbis, with almost every major Jewish urban center throughout the United States having been served at one time or another by at least one of the Hecht brothers.

Rabbi Abraham Hecht had a varied and well-travelled education, having followed in the footsteps of his father, who was sent at the age of 12 to learn in Meah Shearim in Israel for six years. Rabbi Abraham started off in Torah Vodaath in Brooklyn and at the direction of T.V.'s illustrious founder, Reb Shraga Feivel Mendelowitz, ztl, was one of the first 10 bochurim from Torah Vodaath to join the initial class of the Lubavitcher Yeshiva in the United States.

In 1939, he continued his Lubavitch studies in Otwosk, Poland, directly under the last Lubavitcher Rebbe, ztl, but his sojourn didn't last there too long, due to the outbreak of World War II.

Returning to America, he was ordained at the Lubvitcher Yeshiva Rabbinical College and married the former Liba Greenhut.

It was then that he began his travels, but this time as an educator, rather than as a student, to improve the quality of religious life throughout the United States. He was the founder of yeshivos in Newark, New Haven, Buffalo, Worcester and Dorchester. When he return to New York, he became a day school principal and the rabbi of B'nei Magen David Congregation.

He used his talents to establish publications, employment agencies, organize classes, lecture series, book drives and again to set up educational centers and institutions.

In the past 30 years, most of this work was done with the Sephardic community, who came to accept and love this Ashkenaz as one of their own. In 1958, he was named the head of the large and prestigious Shaare Zion Congregation, which he helped build and today it boasts of having a membership of over 1000 families.

In outside work, too, Rabbi Hecht has exhibited boundless energy. He has often visited Israel and has served as the president of the Rabbinical Alliance of America, the Rabbinical Board of Flatbush, as well as on a Presidential conference on children. He has taken an active part in local politics, and has, ironically, attended functions all over the world as THE representative of his Sephardic community.

In the field of publication, he first made his mark 11 years ago with a widely acclaimed book of essays and sermons called "Spiritual Horizons."

It is rather fitting that he continues with something "Spiritual" now, with the recent printing of "Spiritual Freedom", a collection of some of his most prophetic and analytical sermons of the past 10 years.

Congressional Record

House of Representatives

PROCEEDINGS AND DEBATES OF THE 94th CONGRESS, FIRST SESSION

United States of America

Vol. 121   WASHINGTON, FRIDAY, DECEMBER 5, 1975   *No. 179*

Congressional Record

United States of America

PROCEEDINGS AND DEBATES OF THE 98*th* CONGRESS, SECOND SESSION

Vol. 130   WASHINGTON, WEDNESDAY, FEBRUARY 8, 1984   No. 13

Senate

SENATE CONCURRENT RESOLUTION 94—RELATING TO JEWISH EMIGRATION FROM SYRIA

Mr. MOYNIHAN submitted the following concurrent resolution; which was referred to the Committee on Foreign Relations:

S. CON. RES. 94

Whereas the Syrian Government has forbidden all members of the Syrian Jewish community to emigrate;

Whereas the approximately 4,500 Jews living in Syria have been victims of a systematic anti-Jewish, anti-Zionist program, which has included severed restrictions on travel abroad, loss of the right to hold government jobs, laws requiring that all Jews bear special identification cards, and restrictions on Jewish rights of inheritance;

Whereas recent events, including the unexplained murders of a young Syrian Jewish woman and her children, suggest a renewed pattern of violence against the Jews in Syria; and

Whereas Syrian President Hafez Assad stated in a 1976 interview that he would allow the members of the Syrian Jewish community to emigrate to the United States: Now, therefore, be it—

Resolved by the Senate (the House of Representatives concurring), That it is the sense of Congress that the president of Syria should immediately permit all members of the Syrian Jewish community to emigrate from Syria to the United States.

● Mr. MOYNIHAN. Mr. President, today, close to 5,000 Syrian Jews are living in constant fear for their lives. On December 28, 1983, in the town of Aleppo, a Jewish mother, Lillian Adabi, and her two young children were brutally murdered and their bodies mutilated. In a nation ruled by terror, this appalling crime is not so much a matter for law enforcement officials as a message deliberately sent.

The atrocity at Aleppo is only the most recent outrage perpetrated against the Syrian Jewish community. They live in constant fear of harassment and assault, yet they cannot leave. Jews in Syria are forbidden to emigrate, a denial of a basic right recognized by civilized nations the world over and one enjoyed by all other groups in Syria. In March 1974, two Jewish men were murdered and four young Jewish women were raped and killed after attempting to flee Syria for Lebanon.

Also Jews are the object of official discrimination in Syria. Syrian law requires that all Jews carry special identification cards stamped "Musawi"—followers of Moses. No other community in Syria is so identified by religion. To travel abroad -if permitted at all—Jews must post bonds equivalent to $5,000 and leave members of their immediate family behind, like hostages, to guarantee their return. Syrian authorities cruelly have ignored appeals for family reunions with relatives in other nations.

25,000 Jews of Syrian origin live in the United States. Many members of this community have offered to provide homes to the Jews of Syria, should they ever be permitted to emigrate.

We have come to expect brutality from Syria's President Hafez Assad and from his brother Rifaat, the chief of Syria's internal security forces. We have watched this regime murder indiscriminately for decades. In recent months, Americans have experienced the ruthlessness of the Assads in Lebanon—at great cost of American life. Our own experiences with the current Syrian regime ought to make us especially sensitive to the fear and isolation of the Syrian Jewish community.

The awful killing of the Adabi family in Aleppo has added new urgency to the plight of Syrian Jews. The danger to them is real and present.

On January 31, 1984, I spoke at a "Community Wide Rally to Save Syrian Jewry" held by members of the Sha are Zion Congregation in Brooklyn, N.Y., to focus attention on the conditions facing Syrian Jews. The distinguished Governor of New York, my friend Mario M. Cuomo, issued a proclamation designating January 31, 1984, as "Save Syrian Jewry Day" in New York.

Mr. President, the Syrian Jewish community is one of the oldest Jewish communities on Earth. We cannot stand by silently as the Jews of Syria, who have suffered for so many years, are persecuted and murdered. I have introduced a concurrent resolution calling on the President of Syria immediately to permit all members of the Syrian Jewish community to emigrate from Syria. I invite my colleagues in the Senate to join me in support of this humanitarian appeal.

I ask unanimous consent that the Proclamation of the Governor of New York be printed in the RECORD.1

There being no objection, the proclamation was ordered to be printed in the RECORD, as follows:

PROCLAMATION

The Jews in Syria, numbering some 4,000 souls, have been living in constant fear, experiencing discrimination and deprived of their basic and elemental rights as citizens of their country.

They have been subjected to acts of violence and terrorism and denied the universally recognized right to emigrate.

A community-wide rally is being organized in support of their human rights on Tuesday, January 31, 1984.

Now, therefore, I, Mario M. Cuomo, Governor of the State of New York, do hereby proclaim January 31, 1984, as

SAVE SYRIAN JEWRY DAY

In New York State, and I join with the Syrian Jewish community of New York and with all citizens of New York State in requesting unrestricted emigration of Syrian Jews to countries of their choice and the protection of the security, safety and human rights of those Jews who choose to remain in Syria.

I appeal to President Hafez Assad of Syria to meet these humanitarian requests on behalf of Syrian Jews.●

INTERNATIONAL CONFERENCE FOR THE FREEDOM OF JEWS IN SYRIA

organized by SIONA

UNDER THE AEGIS OF THE WORLD SEPHARDIC FEDERATION

AND THE SPONSORSHIP OF

The American Jewish Committee,
The Anti-Defamation League of B'nai Brith,
The Representative Council of Jewish Institutions in France,
The World Jewish Congress.

You are cordially invited to participate in the

INTERNATIONAL CONFERENCE FOR THE FREEDOM OF JEWS IN SYRIA

To be held

SUNDAY, NOVEMBER 18, 1984, from 10:00 to 6:00

at the Hotel PLM St. Jacques
17, Boulevard St. Jacques - 75014 PARIS.

Under the Chairmanship of Mr ALAIN POHER, President of the French Senate

with the participation of :
Chief Rabbi of France René Samuel SIRAT, the Rev. Father RIQUET, Rav. Abraham HECHT,
Amb. Ovadia SOFFER, Jean POPEREN, André MERIC, Simone VEIL, François LEOTARD,
Nissim GAON, Edgar BRONFMAN, Kenneth BIALKIN, Théo KLEIN, Arié L. DULZIN,
Moshe LANDAU, Rika ZARAI, Steve CHALOM, Roger PINTO, Guy BEART, Fernando ARRABAL,
André LWOFF, Alex JOFFE, Jean FERNIOT, Jean PIERRE-BLOCH
and other outstanding personalities.

Facing Opposition

Caustic comments regarding the controversial wording of the Law of Return traveled along the Orthodox grapevine. "Mi hu Yehudi?" was a question begging to be answered, yet its clear-cut response was clouded in smoky puffs of assimilation. The Jewish world had begun responding to this oft-repeated question in an absurd manner that would have elicited a laugh if the situation had not been so dire.

"Who is a Jew?"

"One who says he is!"

This sarcastic exchange was repeated in various forms at countless gatherings and rallies to effectively elucidate the gravity of the situation. The protective gates surrounding our nation were in danger of being demolished, yet no one seemed inclined to keep them erect. How could some of our own brothers in Eretz Yisroel willingly expose the collective Jewish family to insidious influences? Had their perverted views actually pulled the blinds over the most significant aspects of our nation's survival?

At first, I figured that the powerful and influential Jews running the Israeli government were simply unaware of future repercussions. Ignorant as they were in the basic dictates of Yiddishkeit, they probably couldn't fathom why the Orthodox communities were expending so much energy to amend a single word in the innocuous Law of Return. Further investigation unveiled the uncomfortable facts.

Most of the Knesset members were in favor of omitting the word "kehalacha", as were many of the country's respected leaders. The voice of the Chareidim was raised in vehement protest, but the painful issue proceeded steadily along its destructive path. If the shameful train would not be derailed, its journey would continue generating mayhem at an alarming rate.

Pressure had to be applied in the highest echelons of the Israeli political arena in order to achieve desirable results. A strongly-worded letter was dispatched to Golda Meir, Prime Minister of Israel, urging her to reconsider her erroneous decision.

"In connection with the proposed amendment to the "Who is a Jew" law, to be voted on in the near future, we call on you, Prime Minister of Israel...to bring this tragic law, that has brought chaos and splintering amongst Jews throughout the world, to an end...

"...You have accepted a law that any sort of conversion certificate that will be brought from abroad will be accepted...The framework of the Jewish people is eternal. When you declare that by the mere presentation of a worthless piece of paper one is recognized in Israel as a Jew, abolishing the basic criteria of conversion, you simultaneously abolish the very fabric and unity of our people."

I signed off under the title of the Rabbinical Council of the Syrian Community, hoping that my official position would give my words additional clout. My next targets were several Knesset members who would eventually cast their votes on this fateful issue. Joseph Burg, Rabbi Shlomo Lawrence, Yitkah Peretz and Rabbi M. Porush were some of the lucky recipients of my provocative mailgrams. The letters were sent to the Knesset, addressed in their names, accompanied by my warmest prayers for the ultimate success.

The mailgrams read as follows:

We send you this challenge: ad matai *will you block the*

passage of the change in the Mi Yehudi *law. American Jewry is distressed by your apathy and indifference to the problem of intermarriage and assimilation caused indirectly by the law as it now exists. We urge you to take immediate constructive action to amend the law to read "kehalacha".*

Our thanks in advance,

The Rabbinical Alliance of America (i.e. Igud Harabbanim)

Rabbi Abraham B. Hecht, President

Letters, telegrams and mailgrams were ammunition to fight the senseless decree, but there were still many other strategies waiting to be explored. Whatever could not be expressed in inanimate words and sentences would be loudly proclaimed at demonstrations, gatherings and mass rallies. The voice of American Jewry would echo loudly in the hallowed corridors of the Knesset building, exerting necessary pressure on its diversified membership.

Most of these assemblies were organized in New York, under the respected auspices of the Igud Harabbanim. As the president of the organization, I repeatedly directed, chaired and lectured at these significant gatherings. The flames of fear and outrage furiously urged me on to accept greater responsibilities and further commitments. Several times, I was asked to speak at similar assemblies in distant cities, either under the banner of the American Rabbinical Alliance or as the leader of my Sephardic congregation. Traveling from a rally in Beth Israel of Miami to the Igud Harabbanim Convention and all the meetings between the two, I found myself gathering strength with each additional undertaking. While I was stationed on the battlefield to defend Klal Yisroel, there was no thought of retreating to safer territory.

One convention, in particular, warrants mention, due to its widely-acclaimed success. On May 10, 1981, more than two thousand Jews assembled in the Beth Medrash Hagadol of Boro Park. The inclement weather conditions deterred no one from their righteous task, and the pulsating feelings of warmth and purpose infused the walls with a life of their own. Tehillim was recited in unison, followed by a heartfelt Mincha prayer. As Chairman of the Conference, I ascended the podium to describe and convey the importance of the day's mission.

I brought up the Mesiras Nefesh of our parents and grandparents in the Holocaust, who had survived the most sadistic tortures in order to establish future generations.

"For this they had Mesiras Nefesh?" I thundered passionately. "That the Land of Israel should disregard and belittle the procedures of belonging to the Jewish people? That our children and grandchildren should become the victims of dissolution and assimilation?"

As my words echoed in the silence of the crowded shul, I saw the faces of the six million sacrifices that had been consumed by the flames of the Divine Plan. Their accusing stares were akin to piercing swords pointed towards the irreverent leaders of the Jewish State. Our grandparents had offered their lives for their Creator, yet their offspring had no compunctions about defiling their superior lineage. Where was the logical reasoning in this ongoing saga? Would the truth manage to creep out from between the heavy curtains of falsehood?

The conference continued with the inspirational lectures of Hagaon Rav Simcha Elberg, Rav Pinchus Hirshprung and Rav Ephraim Yolles. After listening intently to the fiery speeches, the attendees solemnly exited the shul, infused with passionate conviction.

cans formed to call world attention to the plight of Jews in Middle East countries and headed by General Lucius D. Clay, released an alarming report on the status of Syrian Jews. The report revealed that the ruthless Syrian Government has placed a total ban on Jewish emigration and that 12 young Jews have been imprisoned, charged with attempting to flee the country.

Of these 12 victims of harassment, three are members of a single family: 27-year-old Azur Blanga, his 24-year-old wife and their 4-year-old son. Two are members of another family: Isaac Hamra and Sheila Hamra. The list includes two men besides those mentioned: Abdo Saadia and Simon Bissou. Four unmarried women are among these Jewish prisoners: Badio Dibbo, Miss Boukehi, Miss Meiles and Miss Yachar. The name of the 12th victim is not known.

In addition, the relatives of these 12 Syrian Jews have been taken into custody and interrogated under torture. It is clear from this torture of the prisoners' relatives that Syria's totalitarian dictators are continuing the practice of guilt by association.

Moreover, all Jewish prisoners that have been released from Syrian jails were subjected during their confinement to various forms of savagery at the hands of their Syrian captors. These included electrical torture, the ripping off of fingernails and other types of brutality.

The Committee of Concern's report also revealed that the Jewish cemetery in Damascus has been almost completely

IN THE COMMUNITY OF NATIONS

The SPEAKER. Under a previous order of the House, the gentleman from New York (Mr. PODELL) is recognized for 30 minutes.

Mr. PODELL. Mr. Speaker, just as there are individuals who by their acts become outlaws, so there are also nations which by their cruel policies and inhuman actions violate all accepted norms of international behavior.

During the 1930's and early 1940's, ... to the insane

... systematically slaughtering 6 ... Nazi ...

... More recently, the Soviet ..., adhering to the atheistic Marxian ... of dialectical materialism, has ... and oppressed its Jewish ... struggling to maintain its religious heritage against Russia's Communist dictators.

... I rise to speak out against the ... of another outlaw nation, an dictatorial regime, which is guilty of committing crimes against humanity terrorizing its small Jewish community. The criminal nation to which I refer is Israel's bellicose neighbor to the east, Syria.

The Syrian regime is mercilessly persecuting the 4,000 remaining Jews within its borders in a program of relentless physical and psychological torment. This is the same Syrian regime which races through the most menacing powder keg the Balkans in 1914, uttering cloud, ish shouts, waving torches, throwing lighted matches around and calling for war against Israel.

This is the same Syrian regime which is a Soviet satellite in the Middle East having allowed Russia to utilize ... as a naval base. This is the same Syrian regime that has offered sanctuary to guerrilla skyjackers, insolently contravening international air convention and daring the United States to do something about it.

Earlier this month, the Committee of Concern, a nonsectarian group of Ameri-

fenseless Jewish minority in many ... ways

houses and when a Jew dies, his property is confiscated by the state. Syrian authorities have turned over homes in the Jewish quarter to occupation by Palestinian Arabs who harass the remaining Jewish residents.

Jewish schools have been taken over by the state and Moslem principals appointed.

Jews are barred from practicing in most professional fields.

Within Syria, travel by Jews is restricted to 3 kilometers from one's home address. The ban on travel even extends to needed visits for medical treatment. In contrast to this restriction on Jewish travel, 500,000 Moslem Syrians have crossed the border and visited Lebanon during this year alone.

All Syrian Jews are forced to carry distinctive Jewish identity cards marked with a red stamp, "Member of the Mosaic Faith."

A Higher Committee for Jewish Affairs in the Syrian Ministry of the Interior maintains a constant surveillance over the Jewish community, carrying out frequent arrests and sudden house raids at night.

The Committee of Concern has urged that the barbaric treatment of the Jewish community at the hands of the Syrian regime be brought before the United Nations Commission on Human Rights. If their response is that this treatment of the Jewish minority is "an internal

matter," then my reply, that of the Committee of Concern and that of scholars and plain-thinking citizens of our one world is that this is the same thing that Hitler said when his persecution of the Jews was questioned.

Tyrants in every part of the world, from time immemorial, have proclaimed their perverted theory that what they do to their own people is wholly their own business and that outsiders should keep their prying noses out of what the tyrants have declared to be exclusively "an internal matter." But the truth is that no nation is an island. Humanity is indivisible. Brutality exercised anywhere inevitably wounds the heart and soul of good men everywhere.

That this truth is not universally acknowledged is a tragedy of our epoch in human history. Indeed, the 20th century will be the subject of close scrutiny by future historians for the bureaucratization of evil, and the slowness of neighboring societies and governments to get involved, that have characterized our age. Too often, our era has been marked by morally bankrupt leaders and misled masses committing cruel and inhuman crimes against oppressed minority groups while the world passes by.

To the Syrian tyrants committing these anti-Jewish atrocities, the answer of the U.S. Government, and the answer of all Americans as individuals, should be loud and clear: In the name of humanity, stop. In the name of decency, reconsider. In the name of conscience, reflect on what you are doing. Mankind everywhere, today, is judging you. The ... will judge you ...

The admission and retention of a na... ... subject of recent deliberation throughout the world. If the United Nations is to serve as a truly effective international forum, then it cannot ignore the barbarous actions of the Syrian regime. The United Nations Commission on Human Rights cannot overlook the sadistic brutality of the Syrian Government in persecuting its Jewish minority. I urge the commission to begin immediately a thorough investigation of the torture now occurring in Syria and that the member nations impose the strongest possible economic and political sanctions on the despotic Syrian Government.

STEPHEN J. SOLARZ
13TH DISTRICT, NEW YORK

COMMITTEES
FOREIGN AFFAIRS
CHAIRMAN, SUBCOMMITTEE ON ASIAN
AND PACIFIC AFFAIRS

JOINT ECONOMIC COMMITTEE

EDUCATION AND LABOR

POST OFFICE AND CIVIL SERVICE

WASHINGTON OFFICE:
1536 LONGWORTH HOUSE OFFICE BUILDING
WASHINGTON, DC 20515
(202) 225-2361

DISTRICT OFFICES:
532 NEPTUNE AVENUE
BROOKLYN, NY 11224
(718) 372-8800
619 LORIMER STREET
BROOKLYN, NY 11211
(718) 706-6603
356 COURT STREET
BROOKLYN, NY 11231
(718) 802-1400

Congress of the United States
House of Representatives
Washington, DC
November 25, 1987

Rabbi Abraham B. Hecht
Congregation Shaare Zion
2030 Ocean Parkway
Brooklyn, NY 11223

Dear Rabbi Hecht:

I gather your meeting with Ambassador Okun went well.

I'm pleased you were able to meet with him and that he was responsive to your recommendations.

I only hope you won't hesitate to let me know if there's ever any other way I can be helpful in the future.

Cordially,

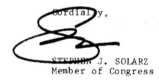

STEPHEN J. SOLARZ
Member of Congress

SJS:vg

A Disastrous Conclusion

ounds of correspondence from the religious communities of America, as well as public rallies and gatherings, placed great pressure on Israel's governing body. Years passed in turmoil while the amendment was pending, yet nothing substantial was accomplished. Orthodox Jewry voiced its demands but we weren't the only soldiers on the battlefield. Directly contesting our every move and aborting our attempts for success, the Reform and Conservative communities staunchly held their ground. Under no circumstances were they prepared to surrender the battle for Klal Yisroel's continuity. If the word "kehalacha" would be added to the Law of Return, any conversions orchestrated by their unscrupulous rabbis would be illegitimate.

Thus, it came as no surprise when virulent articles began appearing in various newspapers. The assimilated American Jews felt threatened by our unstinting efforts, and they employed all their resources to deflect our influence. Ridiculous statements were publicized in their name to prevent the amendment of the Chok Hashvus. According to their nonsensical views, the issue of proper conversion is a point of contention. The Orthodox Jews should not be given free rein in the Israeli government only because they happen to be correct, halachically.

Upon hearing the baseless arguments of the Bnei Brith organization, I immediately penned a letter to two of its leaders.

"We were shocked to read that your organization was one of the prime movers in the opposition to amend the Law of Return on converts. We have always maintained that Bnei Brith is and should be concerned with Jews, as the name implies – Bnei Brith – sons of the covenant.

"...We are trying to protect the integrity of the Jewish people, and we therefore protest vehemently your involvement in a purely religious issue for which you are neither competent nor authorized to make statements.

"Your involvement has caused much misunderstanding throughout the U.S.A. and has promoted a groundswell of protest in our community. We feel that you should disassociate yourselves at once, and publicly, from the group..."

I had previously been privileged to become acquainted with Reform and Conservative obstinacy, so my letter was posted without any high expectations. The straying sheep had rebelled against their Merciful Shepherd and they seemed content with their unacceptable position. Unfortunately, Bnei Brith and its cronies possessed a loud voice and even louder pockets. Their opinions were broadcasted worldwide, and their money was forwarded to the necessary places. Many Knesset members and Israeli leaders bowed respectfully to their erroneous statements and opposed the stipulation of proper conversion.

The United Jewish Appeal of New York also caused much undue anguish. This esteemed organization gathered funds for poor, indigent Jews who sorely depended on the financial assistance. Like so many others at the time, the UJA fell prey to the trap of ignorance and assimilation set by the Israeli government. Aroused by the tumultuous debates being conducted year after year in the Knesset, the UJA self-righteously began its own political campaign to omit the word "kehalacha" from the Chok Hashvus. Money was no issue, for they constantly received sizable donations for our needy Jewish brethren.

I was outraged at their unabashed deviation from true Yiddishkeit, but experience had shown that logical debate would be futile. Assimilated Jews, or those identifying with Reform and Conservative congregations, were simply uninterested in the demands of the Torah. Their pleasures couldn't be curtailed due to teachings they didn't understand or appreciate. Therefore, I chose to focus on another bothersome aspect of the UJA's political efforts.

"…Your use of UJA Federation funds for political purposes, petition drives, political media advertisements here, in the U.S.A. and Israel, is a betrayal of the trust of the majority of contributors who want their money used for humanitarian, and not political, machinations," I wrote to the executive vice presidents.

The erstwhile organization was supposed to use contributed funds for Jews undergoing financial crises and not to further their political campaigns. Money was spent on printing flyers, sponsoring trips to Israel and other political activities that were intended to influence world opinion in their favor. Since a discussion about Klal Yisroel's special status would not make the slightest impression, I focused on their alleged money mismanagement instead.

My words evoked an immediate response from the UJA leaders, who tried to whitewash their untoward actions. I received a harshly-worded mailgram in which the UJA leaders unleashed a tirade of outrage at my accusations. Their fury found expression in that explosive document, as they employed every method of self-defense they could possibly contrive.

"In your advertisement you claim that you represent all the Jewish nonpolitical organizations. We ask you — who appointed you or authorized you to claim to speak in the name of millions of Jews in America?" they wrote in agitation. "Did you conduct a poll? Did you send out a questionnaire? How do you know that you are representing the honest opinion of American Jews?"

After throwing their baseless accusations, they proceeded to outline some uncompromising demands.

"We insist in the name of truth, decency and democracy that you immediately cease the devious announcements in the Israeli press which tend to confuse the issues and misrepresent the truth... You have no right to involve the UJA Federation in this issue..."

The organization was outraged at the accusation I had hurled, but my efforts were rewarded with a modicum of success. When the UJA realized that I wouldn't back down, they were forced to withdraw their support on this painful issue.

This battle was just another spoke in the wheels of the Law of Return. Despite our tireless efforts, the controversy raged on for more than three decades. Sparks of fire can be easily subdued, but a full-blown conflagration is difficult to control. The illogical flames attack anything in their path, without discriminating between good and evil.

The battles raged on without anyone gaining the upper hand. The ball was thrown back and forth, leaving the contestants exhausted and disillusioned. While the issue was being discussed, non-Jews freely entered Eretz Yisroel, hiding behind the worthless conversion certificates. A bogus rabbi's official stamp ensured smooth entry and adjustment, as well as certain benefits and privileges extended to all Jewish immigrants.

Recently, the painful issue was resolved, causing more anguish than all of our battles combined. The Knesset officially decreed that the word "kehalacha" would not be added to the Law of Return. An unsightly hole has been cruelly ripped in the fabric of Klal Yisroel by ignorant and foolish tailors. It is a hole from within, making it extremely difficult to repair. Thirty years ago, we started battling their merciless shears, but the amateur tailors won the war. Their victory, in actuality, is everyone's defeat.

New House
67-68 Hatton Garden
London EC1N 8JY

Tel: 01 580 9146
Tlx: 895 0055

CONFIDENTIAL

13 February 1985
(Dictated in January 1985)

Rabbi Abraham B. Hecht,
Congregation Shaare Zion,
2030 Ocean Parkway,
Brooklyn NY 11223,
U.S.A.

Dear Rabbi Hecht,

Thank you for your letter dated 3 January and for your helpful comments.
On advice from a U.N. specialist I shall not for precedural reasons at the
present time, be pursuing my proposal to instigate a case involving our
brethren through the U.N. Committee, as there is a possible alternative
route which is being explored. Current information is also that Rabbi
Hamra does not want a spate of letters personally (although festive greetings
would not go amiss from time to time).

A journalist to whom I gave contacts has just returned and those to whom
he spoke (he was especially requested to ask the question) would welcome
the issue of their plight being in the public arena. My information on
daily life there roughly corresponds with yours. I did not think it was
wrong for the Paris Conference to take place with attendant publicity
but in my work I avoid any attacks on the regime except insofar as human
rights are generally concerned and their refusal to comply with the U.N.
Declaration of Human Rights.

We do have telephone contact with friends there and are kept informed
about the situation and it would be useful if you and I were to compare
notes from time to time, especially if anything major is brewing.

With every good wish in your work,

Yours sincerely,

MARTIN SHAW
President CHAIRMAN J. Tamman K.St.J.,   Chairman: Martin Shaw.

STEPHEN J. SOLARZ
13TH DISTRICT, NEW YORK

COMMITTEES:
FOREIGN AFFAIRS
CHAIRMAN, SUBCOMMITTEE ON AFRICA
BUDGET

Congress of the United States
House of Representatives
Washington, D.C. 20515

WASHINGTON OFFICE:
1530 LONGWORTH HOUSE OFFICE BUILDING
WASHINGTON, D.C. 20515
(202) 225-2361

DISTRICT OFFICES:
1628 KINGS HIGHWAY
BROOKLYN, NEW YORK 11229
(212) 965-5100

253 BRIGHTON BEACH AVENUE
BROOKLYN, NEW YORK 11235
(212) 965-5105

December 20, 1979

Dear Rabbi Hecht:

It was really good to have you with us here in Washington a short while ago.

I've gotten so many favorable comments from my colleagues on your prayer that I think we could even elect you, if you're interested, as the permanent Rabbi of the House, when we convene next year.

I'm enclosing a copy of the Congressional Record with both your invocation as well as the statement which I made on the Floor of the House paying tribute to you for your many good works and accomplishments. I'm also enclosing a copy of the picture which was taken when we met with the Majority Leader, Jim Wright, in the Speaker's Office shortly before the session began.

I'm looking forward to seeing you shortly after I return from my next mission to the Middle East and to reporting to your congregation on the status of the Jewish community in Syria as well as the prospects for peace in the Middle East at that time.

Cordially,

STEPHEN J. SOLARZ

SJS:vg

Enclosures

Meeting Foreign Dignitaries

I traveled to Eretz Yisroel seven times for various reasons. Each trip was a unique experience that left me anxiously awaiting my next journey. The otherworldly essence of the Holy Land washed over me each time anew, surprising me with its intensity and tangible beauty. During each visit to Israel, I was privileged to meet numerous world personalities and leaders, who graciously shared their opinions and ideals with me.

YITZCHOK BEN ZVI, THE SECOND PRESIDENT OF ISRAEL

The topic we discussed at length was the controversy over a treasured, ancient manuscript written by Ben Asher. The "Keter", titled by the Rambam as the most authentic Sefer Torah in those times, was courageously smuggled out of Syria and brought to Eretz Yisroel. The FaHam family, a well-respected and influential Syrian family unit, masqueraded as simple Arab shepherds hauling some luggage. No one suspected that their bulky packages were simply a foil for the treasured manuscript, and their journey progressed without any mishaps. Thus, at great personal risk, they succeeded in rescuing the priceless Torah scroll and handing it over to the Israeli government.

The FaHam family subsequently immigrated to the United States and settled down in the Syrian community in Brooklyn. After establishing their home in the unfamiliar land, the "Keter" once again occupied their thoughts. They desperately wanted to return the manuscript to its rightful place, among Jews of Syrian descent, but their requests were repeatedly rebuffed. The Israeli government argued that this treasured piece of Jewish history unquestionably belongs in the land of the Jews. Despite their untiring efforts and impassioned pleas, the Keter remained in Eretz Yisroel. At present, the ancient Sefer Torah is encased in a glass container in the Israeli National Museum, for all to see and admire.

Menachem Begin, Prime Minister of Israel

Prior to one of my trips to Eretz Yisroel, the Lubavitcher Rebbe entrusted me with a specific mission. He asked me to visit Menachem Begin and convey the Rebbe's immense pleasure at his efforts concerning the issue of Mihu Yehudi. The Prime Minister had delivered a very powerful address in the Knesset, advocating the amendment of the Chok Hashvus. Being deeply involved in this devastating problem, the Rebbe wished to thank the Israeli leader for courageously promoting the proper course of action.

The first thing on my agenda upon arriving in Israel was to fulfill the Rebbe's request. I found my way to the Knesset building where I asked to see the Prime Minister. Menachem Begin was sitting in the Knesset lunchroom while a tight-lipped security guard stood stiffly at the entrance. As soon as I mentioned the purpose of my visit, the lunchroom doors were thrown open and I was respectfully ushered inside.

"I have a message for you from the Lubavitcher Rebbe," I told the Prime Minister.

The words had barely left my mouth, when Mr. Begin jumped up and stood at attention. His esteemed position notwithstanding, the leader of Israel wanted to show respect for a Torah giant. Amazed at this open display of reverence, I carefully conveyed the Rebbe's warm regards and words of gratitude. The Prime

Minister was obviously greatly moved and impressed, expressing his feelings without reservation.

ZALMAN SHAZAR, PRESIDENT OF ISRAEL

My visit to President Zalman Shazar was also connected with the Mihu Yehudi controversy. I pleaded with the president to amend the Law of Return, citing the disastrous ramifications it could have on the Jewish nation.

"Rabbi Hecht," Shazar responded, "did you see who left my office before you entered?"

"Yes, of course I did. That was the Chief Ashkenazic Rabbi, Rabbi Shlomo Goren," I replied, baffled by his strange question.

"Precisely. Why don't you go to him? After all, he's a respected religious leader here in Israel. Rabbi Goren could certainly assist you in these religious matters more than a secular head of state."

His proposal caught me completely by surprise, but I wasn't ready to accept it. As the president of Israel, Zalman Shazar's opinion carried a lot of clout in the echelons of the governing body.

"Whenever I sought to achieve anything, I've accustomed myself to go directly to the head, and hardly ever to the tail," I explained passionately.

"If you want something important to be done, go to the top. Never waste precious time with a low tier employee. I believe that when lifting a stick or a cane, one should grasp the head of the object and the bottom will automatically come up. So, too, in this very problematic issue, we need the personal intervention of the President. You carry enough political clout to get the Knesset to approve the addition of the word 'kehalacha'."

I fell silent, anxiously awaiting Mr. Shazar's reaction to my heated argument. To my extreme relief, he seemed pleased with my explanation and pledged to apply pressure on the parties involved.

YITZCHOK SHAMIR, PRIME MINISTER OF ISRAEL

I once invited Prime Minister Shamir to visit our Sephardic community during one of his trips to America. His busy schedule and endless political meetings were certain to overshadow my impetuous request, yet I felt that the Shaarei Zion congregation would greatly benefit from such an unprecedented honor.

A short while after I had invited Yitzchok Shamir, I was notified that he had decided to accept the offer. Overwhelmed with excitement and anticipation, my congregation prepared an ostentatious reception. Hundreds of people lined the streets of Ocean Parkway hours before his planned visit. Their impatience increased with each passing minute, but at last, the anticipated moment arrived.

An impressive slew of police motorcycles, unmarked security cars and regular police vehicles announced the Prime Minister's presence. The Sephardim enthusiastically paid homage to this important head of state, vocally expressing their approval.

Before the erstwhile Prime Minister entered the shul, Israeli and American security agents carefully inspected the entire building. Dogs were brought along to sniff out any possible threats of violence. When the imposing edifice was finally cleared of all suspicion, the entourage made its way indoors. Hundreds of men, women and children were crowded into the lobby and social hall. There was much good-natured jostling before everyone was ready to quiet down and listen to Shamir's speech.

The Prime Minister spoke strongly about the Land of Israel and pledged never to divide Jerusalem. He passionately promised not to close any settlements on the West Bank or relinquish territory to the Arabs, despite political sanctions by the United Nations. His words were hailed with enthusiasm by all participants, and spontaneous standing ovations repeatedly interrupted his oration.

His steadfast attitude and iron-strong policies were admirable, and they left a very favorable impression on my congregants. The visit was the topic of conversation for many long weeks, as each word of the Prime Minister's speech was repeated and analyzed.

Unfortunately, history proved him wrong. At the tragic Madrid conference, Yitzchok Shamir was forced to renege on his promise due to the immense pressure exerted by America and the United Nations. The powerful nations of the world forced him to operate in a manner opposing Israel's best interests.

YITZCHOK NAVON, PRESIDENT OF ISRAEL

I met Mr. Navon with my wife. We were received in the president's house, where we were served refreshments and had a serious discussion about problems in Israel and America. He is a very friendly and intelligent person.

PRESIDENT HERZOG

I met him in his office in Jerusalem. He was a true leader, who was very smart, and he was extremely dedicated to the needs of Israel.

EDGAR J. NATHAN 3RD
230 PARK AVENUE
NEW YORK, N. Y. 10017

January 5, 1976

Rabbi Abraham B. Hecht
Shaare Zion Congregation
2030 Ocean Parkway
Brooklyn, N.Y.   11223

Dear Rabbi Hecht:

      I was very happy to receive the copy
of the remarks of Congressman Solarz, referring to
your leadership in the Sephardic Community. It is
a source of pride to all of us that your achievements are recorded in the proceedings of the
Congress.

      With kindest regards, I am

        Sincerely,

        Edgar J. Nathan, 3rd

ejn/a

MAILGRAM SERVICE CENTER
MIDDLETOWN, VA, 22645
16AM

4-0315698321002 11/16/88 ICS IPMRNCZ CSP JFKB
1 7183760009 MGM TDRN BROOKLYN NY 11-16 0532P EST

RABBINICAL ALLIANCE OF AMERICA
2030 OCEAN PKWY
BROOKLYN NY 11223

THIS IS A CONFIRMATION COPY OF THE FOLLOWING MESSAGE:

7183760009 MGMB TDRN BROOKLYN NY 265 11-16 0532P EST
ZIP
MR LESTER POLLACK
MARRIOTT HOTEL
555 CANAL ST
NEW ORLEANS LA 70140   *use*
WE DEPLORE YOUR ~~YOUTH~~ OF THE ISRAELI PRESS TO VOICE YOUR OPPOSITION
TO THE RELIGIOUS PARTY, YOUR INVOLVING THE UJA AND FEDERATION IN THE
INTERNAL AFFAIRS OF THE JEWISH STATE, AFTER ALL YOU ARE ONLY THE
FINANCIAL CUSTODIAN OF A NATIONAL PHILANTHROPIC ORGANIZATION AND YOU
HAVE NO RIGHT-MORAL OR LEGAL TO CLAIM TO REPRESENT THE VIEW POINTS OF
AMERICAN JEWRY IN THE QUESTION OF WHO IS A JEW, IN YOUR ADVERTISEMENT
YOU CLAIM THAT YOU REPRESENT ALL THE JEWISH NONPOLITICAL
ORGANIZATIONS, WE ASK YOU-WHO APPOINTED YOU OR AUTHORIZED YOU TO
CLAIM TO SPEAK IN THE NAME OF MILLIONS OF JEWS IN AMERICA, DID YOU
CONDUCT A POLL-DID YOU SEND OUT A QUESTIONNAIRE, HOW DO YOU KNOW THAT
YOU ARE REPRESENTING THE HONEST OPINION OF AMERICAN JEWS, WE INSIST
IN THE NAME OF TRUTH, DECENCY, AND DEMOCRACY TO IMMEDIATELY CEASE THE
DEVIOUS ANNOUNCEMENT IN THE ISRAELI PRESS WHICH TEND TO CONFUSE THE
ISSUES AND MISREPRESENT THE TRUTH, IF ANYONE IS GUILTY OF SPLITTING
THE JEWISH NATION IT IS THE REFORM AND CONSERVATIVE MOVEMENT, YOU
HAVE NO RIGHT TO INVOLVE THE UJA FEDERATION IN THIS ISSUE, LET THE
REFORM AND CONSERVATIVE MOVEMENTS SPREAD THEIR OWN BIAS AND
DIVISIVENCE AND NOT HIDE BEHIND THE UJA FEDERATION, WE PLEAD WITH YOU
DON'T DISCREDIT AND DESTROY THE IMPORTANT PHILANTHROPIC ORGANIZATION
help BY GETTING ENMESHED IN ISSUES THAT HAVE NOTHING TO DO WITH FINANCIAL
~~HEALTH~~ FOR JEWS EVERYWHERE,
RABBI ABRAHAM B HECHT RABBINICAL ALLIANCE OF AMERICA
2030 OCEAN PKWY
BROOKLYN NY 11223

17:31 EST

MGMCOMP

Honoring My Yiddishe Mama

RABBI ELI HECHT

As a child I was taught in the Jewish private school I attended, that every day is father's and mother's day. Our teachers quoted the commandment, to honor your father and mother. My European teachers saw no reason for special dedications. Children were expected to revere and honor parents at all times and places. My teacher was fond of quoting a story in the Talmud of a student, Yosef, who, upon hearing the footsteps of his mother, would say "Let me stand up, for the Divine presence is approaching." Respect and love for parents were a given.

I marveled at my mother's super human skills. She arose early in the morning, prepared breakfast for all nine children plus a lunch for school. The night before she would prepare our clothing and our school knapsacks. When we came home there was always hot soup and something to eat. There is a neat saying that can apply to her: "G-d cannot be everywhere, so he created mothers." Mom claimed that each child was special and she had no favorites. She once told me that I should think of myself as her only child and then I would be happy with all the love she would show. She once raised up her hands and counted her fingers "You see, I have 10 fingers, each one is important, each one has a purpose, nine fingers correspond to the nine kids of our home, the 10th finger is papa. Together we make a great important family." Each child was told that they carried a special name. We were all named after some relative who lived in the old country or a great spiritual leader. We were told, "You must bring honor to our name and family."

Growing up in the 1950s money was scarce, but my mother always found a way for us to have what we needed. The soup sometimes tasted a little bit watery but it was

Gedolim in Eretz Yisroel

My frequent visits to Israel allowed me to meet many of the leading political figures in the holiest and most disputed piece of land on our planet. Aside from my appointments with those holding the reins of government, I was also privileged to come in contact with the religious leaders of Eretz Yisroel. As much as the prime ministers and presidents believe in their power to ensure the small country's survival, the true solution lies in other hands. Only the continued efforts of Israel's Chareidim in the areas of Torah study and steadfast Yiddishkeit can stave off our Arabic enemies.

Therefore, I felt extremely privileged to meet with several of the Chief Rabbis in Eretz Yisroel. Their piety and unshakeable faith were a source of strength and support at all times. When the ship was being thrown violently from one Arab crest to another, these fearless captains courageously stayed at the helm, leading the passengers to safety.

RABBI UNTERMAN, CHIEF RABBI OF ISRAEL

I met Rabbi Unterman at his office in a beautiful building in Jerusalem, adjacent to the Great Synagogue. As soon as I entered, I was struck by the aura of holiness and statesmanship that emanated from his impressive visage. His long, flowing beard and tall, dignified stature added to his noble bearing, resulting in an awesome impression of Torah splendor.

Rabbi Unterman graciously invited me to his house, for an amiable, undisturbed conversation. I was astounded at his display of friendship to a new acquaintance, and gladly accepted. When we arrived at our destination, the esteemed Rabbi proceeded to make me feel completely at home.

"What's the problem?" he asked the young attendant. "Is today a fast day that I was never informed about? Why don't you serve some tea and biscuits to our guest from America?"

The valet acknowledged the good-natured request with a slight nod of his head, and immediately set out the suggested refreshments. Our discussion flowed effortlessly from one topic to another, as we analyzed the differences precipitated by our lands of origin. I immensely enjoyed the relaxed and informative conversation with the esteemed Chief Rabbi, and we parted with promises for future contact.

Rabbi Yitzchok Nissim, Chief Rabbi of Israel

One of the most colorful rabbinic personalities I've ever had the pleasure of meeting was the renowned Chief Rabbi Yitzchok Nissim. When Pope Pius once came to visit Israel, several dignitaries urged Rabbi Nissim to visit this religious leader. It was important to forge a positive relationship with this high-ranking Christian leader to forestall future problems. To their consternation, the Chief Rabbi refused to heed their request, citing his reasons staunchly and publicly.

"If a foreign religious dignitary comes to visit Israel, he should show respect for the head religious authority, the Chief Rabbi," he proclaimed heatedly. "Why should I go out to receive him if he doesn't show the minimum respect that should be accorded to the head of the religious community?"

His outspoken, albeit logical, comments caused great controversy amongst the various sects of Israeli society, yet he refused to back down. Ironclad determination and an unshakeable belief in what was correct according to mesorah characterized this man as one worthy of carrying the mantle of leadership.

When Rabbi Yitzchok Nissim made the journey to America, my Sephardic community enthusiastically prepared an elaborate reception. He was hosted in our shul for the Shabbos services, and subsequently delivered a powerful address. Following the speech, we invited him to partake of a beautiful Shabbos meal where cantors entertained the large crowd with traditional Sephardic tunes.

The Chief Rabbi's short visit made a profound impression on the entire congregation. Years later, members of my community commented that when traveling to Israel, they made it a matter of principle to visit Rabbi Yitzchok Nissim after the Shabbos services.

Rabbi Ovadiah Yosef, Chief Rabbi of Israel

As the Sephardic Chief Rabbi, Rabbi Ovadiah Yosef expressed a sincere interest in our community in Brooklyn. He made a point of visiting our shul on Shabbos, generating much excitement and pride amongst my congregants. We visited several day schools and girls' schools together, and attended many receptions. His sharp insights and keen understanding transformed each moment into a valuable learning experience.

At a reception organized by the Rabbinical Alliance of America, the Igud HaRabbanim over which I presided, Rabbi Ovadiah Yosef surprised me with an interesting remark.

"When introducing Rabbi Hecht at any public gathering," he announced, "he should be referred to as Chacham Abraham (the highest honor accorded to Sephardic leaders)!"

Rabbi Mordechai Elyahu, Sephardic Chief Rabbi of Israel

In 1967, I met Rabbi Elyahu who was then a young man already destined for greatness. Our relationship continued for many long years, leading up to his appointment as Chief Rabbi. He frequently visited America in general and our community in particular. Once I was even privileged to host Rabbi Elyahu and his wife for a week, while he made the rounds of several synagogues, yeshivos and seminaries. All who heard his brilliant Torah lectures were amazed at his depth of understanding and unbelievable breadth of knowledge.

One event takes first place for its indisputable significance and spiritual beauty. The Shaarei Zion congregation sponsored a memorable evening in honor of the two Chief Rabbis of Israel. Rabbi Mordechai Elyahu, the Chief Rabbi of the Sephardim, appeared together with Rabbi Kahane, the Ashkenazic Chief Rabbi. It is impossible to adequately describe the impact their mutual respect had on the large crowd. A sense of unity and Kedushah enveloped all attendees, and accompanied them for many long days.

That memorable evening was a strong lesson in Kavod HaTorah, and it gave us a small glimpse of what the world will look like after Moshiach's arrival. Ashkenazim and Sephardim will recognize the inconsequence of their longstanding disputes in the greater scheme of things. Trivial differences will fall away, to be replaced by a unified nation seeking only to glorify the name of Hashem.

RABBI YITZCHOK KHADOURI, OLDEST KABBALIST IN ISRAEL

Rabbi Khadouri was born in Iraq and presently resides in Jerusalem. His holiness and breadth of knowledge in both nigleh and nistar are legendary. Many years ago, Rabbi Khadouri sought the blessing of the Lubavitcher Rebbe for a project that had just gotten underway. A building was being constructed for the purpose of educating a select few individuals in the mystic powers of Kabbalah.

The Rebbe asked his illustrious guest for his full name, and when he received the answer, his face lit up with pleasure. Khadouri, which in Hebrew translates as "a round ball", was the basis of the Rebbe's blessing.

"Just as your name means a round object, so too, should your name be around, all over the world."

A short while after Rabbi Khadouri's visit, his building in Jerusalem reached completion and was ready for use. At present, one hundred married men dedicate their lives to the study of Kabbalah within the four walls of this building. Rabbi Khadouri, as their esteemed teacher, guides them through the intricacies of their studies.

Baba Sali
RELIGIOUS LEADER OF SEPHARDIC JEWRY WORLDWIDE

Meeting Baba Sali was an interesting and uplifting experience, with an exotic Moroccan flavor. When I entered his home, I saw the revered leader sitting cross-legged on a rug, as was the custom in Morocco. I was introduced as the Rabbi of the Syrian community in Brooklyn, and subsequently received an invitation to join Baba Sali for lunch.

Along with another twelve guests, I entered the dining room that was already lavishly prepared for the midday meal. Seated directly across the Moroccan sage, I watched his every move with fascination. I had plenty of time to observe him, for the meal lasted nearly five hours. Several times, I merited saying L'chaim to Baba Sali over a cup of arak, the official drink at his table. Songs were sung with warmth and emotion, and special emphasis was placed on the song of Bar Yochai.

At one point during the meal, I asked the gabbai if Baba Sali could give a personal blessing for the Lubavitcher Rebbe.

"The Rebbe does not need my blessing," the tzaddik replied with a smile. "His blessing is from Hashem."

It's interesting to note that he had never met the Lubavitcher Rebbe, but when he was asked if he knows him, Baba Sali answered in the affirmative.

"Of course I know him," he said. "I meet him daily as he is either leaving or arriving at the heavenly gates of prayer."

The long meal eventually wound to a close, to the chagrin of all those present. Each guest received a personal blessing from the revered Moroccan sage and reluctantly left the room. As I stood respectfully before him, I impulsively requested that he place his hands directly on my head as he uttered his heartfelt berochos. Baba Sali agreed to my unconventional request and blessed me with hatzlocha in all areas. The impressions of that memorable day in Netivot have not dulled with the passage of time, for the intensity of such an experience cannot be forgotten.

tasty and we all were thankful for it. I remember my little brothers and sisters asking my parents, "Why do the older siblings get to wear their clothing first?" Somehow, mom found time to teach us how to be decent kids. We all had chores and were expected to act accordingly. Last but not least, each of us graduated high school and went on to seminary. All five boys became rabbis and teachers, and my four sisters married rabbis and teachers. Our family grew by leaps and bounds enjoying the freedom and opportunities granted by our great country. I always thank G-d for having such a wonderful mother.

Now, my mother is not with us anymore. She passed away this week. I think of the incredible sacrifices all mothers make to bring children into this world. How they selflessly care, doing everything possible for their children. Each child is a diamond, a blessing created by loving parents. I was blessed to have such a wonderful mother. This week, as our family sat Shiva, all nine children are married to rabbis or are rabbis, working to perpetuate Torah and Yiddishkeit. From California to New York, from Detroit, Michigan to Nice, France, we began to realize the wonderful feelings we have for each other. All this came to us naturally, for a loving mother instills love in her children. In times of sorrow and happiness, we all miss our Yiddishe mommas.

MICHAEL LEWAN
2931 South Columbus Street
Arlington, Virginia 22206

December 22, 1982

Rabbi Abraham B. Hecht
Congregation Shaare Zion
2030 Ocean Parkway
Brooklyn, New York 11223

Dear Rabbi Hecht:

I want to take this opportunity to say good-bye and to thank you for all the kindness and cooperation you've shown me over the last eight years.

I consider myself fortunate to have had the privilege to get to know and work closely with you in the effort to better our community and our country.

You will always stand out in my mind as one of the most concerned and compassionate people I've met.

It has been a great honor to serve at your side, and I hope we can remain friends in the future.

Sincerely,

Mike

Michael Lewan
(Executive Assistant
to Cong. Steve Solarz)

Thanks, you're my favorite Rabbi!

Visiting American Leaders

$\mathcal{A}$side from the dignitaries I met in foreign lands, I was privileged to meet many important personalities on American soil.

American presidents I met:

JIMMY CARTER

Accompanied by Congressman Solarz, I met in the White House with him. We presented him with a silver-covered Old Testament. We discussed the problems of Syrian Jewry and the role America could play in convincing the Syrian president, Asad, to allow the Jewish population in Syria to immigrate to countries of their choice.

Years later, as mentioned earlier in the book, my personal efforts combined with political pressure resulted in the complete exit of the community to our Syrian community in Brooklyn, N.Y.

I also met President Ronald Reagen, George Bush and Bill Clinton.

MEETING AT UNITED NATIONS WITH THE THEN SECRETARY KURT WALDHEIM

I organized a committee to meet with Kurt Waldheim, then Secretary General of the United Nations.

I included several representatives from Israel; Syrian Jews who had managed to escape from Syria and established residence in the Holy Land. My purpose was to have Asad allow Jews to rejoin members of their families in a Reunification Effort, thus allowing many families to emigrate to America, Mexico, South America and Europe.

My delegation was received very warmly by the Secretary General and his staff. He listened attentively and promised to do what he could to help Syrian Jews reunite with their families living in countries throughout the world.

When the Israeli delegation sought to inject political issues about Israel, I immediately informed the Secretary General that the issue we came for crossed political lines and that all we wanted was his help to let Syrian Jews emigrate.

An emissary from the Vatican

The Vatican had sent a special emissary to America to find a Rabbi who would be given a position in the Vatican College to teach aspiring young priests the Old Testament in its original Hebrew. The emissary, a young Catholic priest, was directed to Rabbi Joseph Soloveichik of Yeshiva University to ask him to provide a candidate.

The Rabbi knowing of the opposition of the Orthodox community, which he shared, about any ecumenical efforts with the church, declined. However, he recommended that he visit me as president of the Rabbinical Alliance of America and perhaps I could suggest a Rabbi for the position.

The emissary arrived dressed in a black suit with no visible Christian ornaments — just a turned collar. I received him formally and we discussed his mission at length.

I advised him of the ruling of our Rabbis that we are not to enter into any ecumenical activities with the church. I explained to him at length the objection of the heads of our seminaries to his mission. We spent several hours discussing matters affecting the world politics and the role the Vatican could play in ending the war in Israel. I also spent much time convincing him that the

Vatican should exert maximum pressure on the Syrian government to allow for the reunification of families as a purely humanitarian goal.

We became friends and, although disappointed that he
couldn't get his wish granted, he promised that upon his return
to Rome he would speak to the Pope personally.

Incidentally, when the congregation conducted a trip to Israel
for its members, we visited Rome on the way to Israel. I contacted the priest who had visited me, and he came to see me incog-
nito at the hotel in Rome where I was staying with the group.

He assured me of his talk with the Pope and promised that he
would recommend continued efforts on behalf of the Syrian Jewish Community.

VISITING THE RELIGIOUS HEADS
OF THE MARONITE CHURCH IN AMERICA

In my efforts to help save the Syrian community, I made contact with the leader of the Maronite Christians in America. I visited him in the vestry of his church in Bensonhurst.

We had a very satisfying talk. As the religious leader of a
Christian minority residing in the Middle East, he appreciated
the difficult situation of the Jewish minority. I asked him to use
whatever influence he had in the Middle East to help our brethren.

He was very cooperative and he promised to do his utmost to
assist the Jewish community in Syria to leave.

ARCHBISHOP IKAVOS, HEAD OF THE RUSSIAN-TURKISH CHURCH

I had heard that this Archbishop was the head of a large
church population in the Middle East. I therefore called and
made an appointment with him. I met him, not in any church
building, but at his residence.

We had a long discussion in which I shared with him my fears
for the safety of the Syrian Jewish community. He revealed to me

that he had very strong ties with the Vatican. They were trying to effect a coming together, and that he would use his strong influence to provide protection for the Jewish community in Syria.

I believe that he did convey his concerns to the government involved, with the result of better treatment.

OTHER WORLD LEADERS I MET:

In my successful personal efforts to rescue the 4500 souls constituting the Jewish community living in Syria, I had occasion to meet with world leaders.

I made a personal trip to Geneva in 1967 to visit with the High Commissioner for Refugees. My purpose was to advise him that the Jews in Syria were in dire danger of being decimated by the president of Syria, Asad, as a result of the destruction of the Egyptian Air Force and losses of the Arabs in their war against Israel.

We had a very serious conversation as to how we could help save the Jewish community. He was very friendly, courteous and aware of the problem. He promised to do what he could and exert whatever pressure he was able to in order to help.

STEPHEN J. SOLARZ
13TH DISTRICT, NEW YORK

COMMITTEES:
INTERNATIONAL RELATIONS

POST OFFICE AND
CIVIL SERVICE

WASHINGTON OFFICE:

MICHAEL LEWAN
ADMINISTRATIVE ASSISTANT

1530 LONGWORTH HOUSE OFFICE BUILDING
WASHINGTON, D.C. 20515
(202) 225-2361

Congress of the United States

House of Representatives

Washington, D.C. 20515

DISTRICT OFFICES:

KENNETH LOWENSTEIN
DISTRICT REPRESENTATIVE

1628 KINGS HIGHWAY
BROOKLYN, NEW YORK 11229
(212) 965-5100

117 BRIGHTON BEACH AVENUE
BROOKLYN, NEW YORK 11235
(212) 965-5105

April 27, 1978

Rabbi Abraham B. Hecht
Congregation Shaare Zion
2030 Ocean Parkway
Brooklyn, N.Y. 11223

I can't begin to tell you how much I appreciated the hand-baked matzos which you sent me for the Passover holiday.

I thought you would like to know that my wife and I were privileged to have Vice President and Mrs. Mondale as our guests for the first night of the Seder at our home in Virginia and we used the matzo you had sent us for the occasion.

I told the Vice President, by the way, that he would now know, if nothing else, that the conflict between Israel and Egypt didn't begin thirty years ago!

Cordially,

STEPHEN J. SOLARZ
Member of Congress

SJS:cid

STEPHEN J. SOLARZ
13TH DISTRICT, NEW YORK

COMMITTEES:
FOREIGN AFFAIRS
CHAIRMAN, SUBCOMMITTEE ON AFRICA
BUDGET

Congress of the United States

House of Representatives

Washington, D.C. 20515

WASHINGTON OFFICE:
1530 LONGWORTH HOUSE OFFICE BUILDING
WASHINGTON, D.C. 20515
(202) 225-2361

DISTRICT OFFICES:
1628 KINGS HIGHWAY
BROOKLYN, NEW YORK 11229
(212) 965-5100

253 BRIGHTON BEACH AVENUE
BROOKLYN, NEW YORK 11235
(212) 965-5105

December 27, 1979

Rabbi Abraham Hecht
Cong. Shaare Zion
2030 Ocean Parkway
Brooklyn, New York   11223

Dear Rabbi Hecht:

It was really great to have you with us during our meeting with the President at the White House a few days ago.

It was a moving and memorable experience and I must say that it wouldn't have been quite the same without so many of my good friends from Brooklyn being there with me.

I'm really glad you were able to make it, and I'm looking forward to getting together with you back in Brooklyn shortly after my return from my mission to the Middle East in January.

My best wishes for a healthy and happy New Year.

Cordially,

STEPHEN J. SOLARZ
Member of Congress

SJS.1

P.S.   While I realize this isn't the picture you're waiting for, I thought I might enclose this one of us pending the arrival of the other one with the President.

Kashrus Awareness

Throughout the fifty years that I officiated as Rabbi in the Sephardic community, various events, projects and undertakings kept the clock ticking at an accelerated pace. Time seemed to run right past me, leading me on an endless chase, desperately gasping for breath. The merry-go-round was dizzying and extremely exhausting, but, contrary to those decorating carnivals and circuses, my personal journey had a definite, worthy destination. I was dedicated to the spiritual health of my congregants, and any sign of progress was cause for celebration.

Fatigue and exhaustion was a small price to pay for fulfillment and success in community work. Although at first I hadn't realized the full extent of responsibility my job entailed, I willingly accepted the colossal position. Personal considerations had to be greatly compressed and repressed in deference to the needs of Congregation Shaare Zion. My vice-presidential position in the Sephardic Rabbinical Council added an overwhelming amount of work to my daily schedule, as did my appointment as the executive vice-president of our Bais Din.

The number of issues that came up during those years of continuous activity is staggering. They ranged from slightly complicated to seriously complex and confusing. Some problems were easily dealt with, whereas others demanded constant thought and attention. Certain basic concepts of Torah observance had to be enforced with persistence and determination for several years before they were accepted across the board.

Kashrus is a quintessential example of a basic mitzvah that had to fight its way into the community's conscience. For some reason, it had fallen by the wayside many years previous and its gradual resurrection was a complex and sensitive mission. Generally, my congregants were well-aware of the pertinent halachos regarding a product's proper certification but they tended to patronize stores with questionable kashrus standards. Their excuses ranged from mildly interesting to utterly ridiculous, but the facts remained stagnant in all cases. The people didn't want to be bothered with careful, painstaking inspections of the stores and restaurants they preferred. It was decidedly easier to ignore the niggling inner voices urging them to frequent reputable establishments.

As soon as I grasped the enormity of the problem, I started organizing a concerted effort to heighten kashrus awareness in our slumbering community. It's a known fact that the victuals consumed by a Jew have a direct effect on his spiritual condition and sensitivity. It was impossible to ignore the daily transgressions committed by numerous families who were uninformed or unconcerned with the serious consequences of their unacceptable eating habits.

A Kashrus Committee was established under the auspices of the Rabbinical Council for the Syrian communities in America. As the president of this august organization, I was heavily involved in the activities of all sub-committees. Thus, the activities related to kashrus regulations in stores, restaurants and diners passed under my careful scrutiny.

We commissioned several renowned, reputable mashgichim to oversee the operations of each store individually. If the kashrus standards were deemed satisfactory, that particular establishment was awarded our stamp of approval. The mashgichim faithfully remained at their stations, like a battalion of loyal soldiers.

These generals constantly ascertained that the rules were adhered to at all times. If the store owners refused to allow our mashgichim free access to anything pertaining to the matters in question, our sought-after certification was immediately revoked. Rescinding such decisions demanded a lot of goodwill and visible signs of improvement on the part of the guilty proprietor.

From time to time, we printed comprehensive lists of all butcher shops, grocery stores, pizza shops, caterers and bakeries that met with our approval. These lists were subsequently mailed to the members of our community to assist them in making the proper choices. We also sent cover letters to update the congregants on our progress and to reiterate the importance of patronizing reliable establishments. It was important that our community members should understand and internalize the messages we were attempting to transmit.

In May of 1982, we sent out one of the regular kashrus lists, along with a veritable smidgen of information about our monumental efforts.

> *"Dear Constituent,"* the letter read.
>
> *"It is our pleasure to inform you that our Kashrus Commission is continuing its dedicated efforts to bring a cohesive program of Kashrus supervision to all food establishments serving the members of our community. We have been meeting regularly, and we are increasing the visits by our mashgiach to the places listed. Additional improvements are constantly taking place.*
>
> *"We thank you for your cooperation and we respectfully urge you to patronize those stores which we recommend. Please feel free to call for information regarding the Kashrus standards of the stores in which you shop.*
>
> *"We enclose a list of establishments which we feel have adequate supervision. This list supersedes all other lists. If a store*

previously listed is not included in this current list, we cannot recommend its Kashrus."

The lists were received with much appreciation, and garnered a decidedly positive response. Sometimes we were forced to re-voke our kashrus certification from specific shops due to inex-cusable laxity in various aspects of Halacha. One storeowner was informed that if his shop would not be closed at least a half-hour before the onset of Shabbos, we would be forced to remove his establishment from our list. Another owner was warned that if he continued to disrupt the meticulous investigations of our mashgiach, his shop would suffer the same fate.

The proprietors were well aware of the increased sales our coveted kashrus seal generated, and were therefore willing to ac-cede to our demands. Our experienced mashgichim continued to do their work faithfully, and the storeowners learned to accept their criticism and rebuke. The work was painstaking and often unwelcome, but we stubbornly chipped away the granite walls of cynicism and indifference. With the passage of time, the opera-tion gained momentum and stability, leading to widespread ac-ceptance and admiration. The community learned to welcome the information we provided and tried to adhere to the clear-cut regulations.

The most obvious proof of our success were the ever-lengthening lists of stores boasting our kashrus certification. It was gratifying to hear former antagonists clamoring for the ap-proval of our Kashrus Commission. Sellers and buyers alike learned to view this issue in the proper light, thus ensuring their willing assistance and cooperation.

HOUSE OF REPRESENTATIVES

WASHINGTON, D. C. 20515

STEPHEN J. SOLARZ
13TH DISTRICT, NEW YORK

December 11, 1975

Rabbi Abraham Hecht
c/o Shaare Zion
2110 Ocean Parkway
Brooklyn, New York   11223

Dear Rabbi Hecht,

I read with great interest and much
pride Chaim Yerushalme's article on you
in the Jewish Press.

Such a well deserved tribute clearly
merited a wider audience and, in this
regard, I took the liberty of inserting
the article in the Congressional Record.

I have been genuinely impressed by your
good work and I only hope that our bonds of
friendship will continue to grow in the years
ahead.

Best regards!

Cordially,

P.S. Your article appears on page E6470 of
the Congressional Record.

Maintaining our Mesorah

My community work was as complicated as it was varied. Kashrus awareness was seated in the front row for several decades, but, to my chagrin, it wasn't privileged to solitary confinement. A host of other religious ailments brazenly settled themselves in the homes and hearts of my congregants, demanding our attention with an accusing silence.

A second issue of major significance was the alarming increase in the worldwide rate of intermarriage. Assimilation and ignorance played the greatest roles in this vicious epidemic, and a suitable remedy was yet to be discovered. As the spiritual leader of a growing community, the dangers of this plague weighed heavily on my mind. I couldn't allow any sheep to stray from the flock, for they were under my jurisdiction. Sitting complacently and bemoaning the bitter reality was tantamount to offering unbidden assistance in this devilish performance.

The strategy we implemented to sabotage the Satan's malicious plan was considered drastic by most, but there was no better alternative. As the president of the Rabbinic Council for Syrian Jewry in North America, I took the initiative in this life-and-death situation. I knew that I was battling for the indomitable chain of Mesorah. Therefore, I was determined to persevere despite the daunting mound of obstacles placed in my path.

I announced the decision of the Rabbinic Council concerning this sensitive topic. To prevent any possibility of intermarriage in the Sephardic communities, we would be unable to accept any converts into our congregations. We knew that there were many geirim who were righteous and authentic, but we couldn't risk the presence of imposters. It was a drastic step that was pre-empted by a universal disease.

Occasionally, requests for geirus were forwarded to the offices of the Rabbinic Council, but I was forced to respond in the negative. Despite the valid reasoning that backed these petitions, it was impossible to unveil a chink in our steely armor. The slightest crack would prompt a veritable deluge of similar cases and situations, which would ultimately destroy our firm stance.

The Sephardic communities didn't perform any conversions, nor did they accept anyone who had been converted at other locations. Throughout my years as a Sephardic rabbi, I was faced with several instances of flagrant disobedience in this area. Several congregants wished to marry geirim, but I was forced to prevent the realization of their plans.

It wasn't enough to simply threaten and lecture on this life-threatening topic. Drastic measures had to be implemented in order to ensure the continued safety of my community. When I was informed of any transgression, I was forced to mete out immediate penalties despite the painful difficulties such punishments engendered.

Converts and their spouses, as well as their children, were not allowed to purchase permanent seats in shul at any occasion. The gabbai of our large Bais Medrash was ordered to adhere to these regulations under all circumstances. Aside from that, he was asked to abstain from granting them any official honors in shul. Converts, or those who married converts, could not receive an aliyah in any Sephardic synagogue in New York.

The stiff rules were painful to those on both sides of the desk, but the rising intermarriage rates left us with no choice. I knew that there were several righteous gentiles who expressed a genuine desire to join the Jewish people, but we could make no exceptions. A slight breach would reach disastrous proportions in less time than it takes to record its damage.

In conserving the purity of my large congregation, I didn't want to shoulder the blame of obliterating future Jewish generations due to my refusal to accept the conversion of their ancestor. I found comfort in the fact that although the Sephardic communities had accepted this decision as essential to their continuity, most of American Jewry focused on other aspects that demanded rectification. There were plenty of communities in New York who were willing to delve into the intricate rulings concerning each individual conversion. Thus, a ger tzedek was certain to find his place in one of the multiple religious kehillos that abounded in Brooklyn and beyond.

Each time I was forced to turn away from the pleas of a convert, my conviction underwent a severe pounding. I felt my determination give way to deep compassion, but the vision of my community's survival pulled me through at the last minute. With each negative answer, I was literally strengthening the security fence surrounding my congregation. Every time an insincere convert was politely, albeit firmly, turned away, another few bricks were added to the walls of protection.

Most decisions and promises tend to lose their luster with the passage of time, leading to a steady decline in their upkeep. We feared that our stance on conversion would suffer a similar fate if it wasn't enforced and reiterated on a regular basis. The Shabbos Shuva campaign materialized as the shield of our far-reaching campaign.

A letter dated October 6, 1986 elucidated the reasoning behind this novel idea. The letter bore my signature, as the vice president of the Rabbinic Council, and was mailed to the Sephardic rabbis in various communities dotting the United States landscape.

"Several years ago, the rabbis and presidents of all the congregations and institutions in our community signed a procla-

mation against the acceptance of converts. It was then agreed that every year on Shabbos Shuva, all the sermons in the congregations will be devoted to a reaffirmation and discussion of the ramifications of this community proclamation.

"We, therefore, ask you to please dedicate your sermon this Shabbos to an exposition of the problems of intermarriage and assimilation threatening the existence of the American Jewish community...

"It is vitally important that we re-emphasize and reinforce our ruling, which is protecting our community from the ravages of the dreaded disease of intermarriage."

Similar letters were mailed each year to remind the Sephardic rabbis of their commitment. The annual lectures solidified the decision, and assisted in its successful execution.

At times, different letters had to be sent out to specific communities, urging them to remain steadfast in their stance against conversions. If I received notice that a rabbi had granted an aliyah to a convert, I immediately penned a strong rebuke accompanied by words of encouragement in this particular issue. These occasional reminders preserved our decision for many decades, thus greatly minimizing the dangers of intermarriage and assimilation.

The late Chief Rabbi of our community, Rabbi Jacob S. Kussin O.B.M., was the strongest advocate of this ruling which was originally formulated by a great Sephardic sage, Rabbi Sutton, living in South America at the end of the 19th century. This Rabbinic Proclamation was printed and affirmed by the Magen David Congregation, originally on 67th st. Bklyn. It was affirmed again by thirty-one leaders of the Sephardic community of Brooklyn, N.Y. B"h, the community stringently adheres to the rules and regulations regarding converts, and has remained almost completely free of any intermarriage.

Those few who rebelled against these regulations and married converts have been banished from the community.

Brooklyn Synagogue Celebrates Coming Arrival of Syrian Brides

By PRANAY GUPTE

In the shade of huge maples and elms, the Congregation Shaare Zion synagogue is set apart from the aging wood-and-brick homes on Brooklyn's Ocean Parkway by its elegant stone facade, its large glass doors and its smooth marble steps.

Some call it the loveliest synagogue in the borough, and yesterday it was the scene of special rejoicing.

The celebration had to do with the anticipation that soon the temple, which has the biggest Sephardic congregation in Brooklyn, would be welcoming new members—dozens of Syrian Jewish women who are expected to be wed, by proxy, to young men from the community.

The Ocean Parkway area has the single largest concentration of the 40,000 Jews of Syrian origin in the United States—nearly 25,000—and the neighborhood is sometimes called "Little Syria."

"We are delighted that the marriages will take place," Maurice Sutton, one of the synagogue's officials, said yesterday after the morning's Sabbath ceremonies. "This is a time of joy for all of us."

It is also a time of disturbing change for the Syrian Jewish community of Ocean Parkway. Twenty years ago, well-to-do Sephardic Jews of Syrian descent began moving from the Bay Parkway area of Bensonhurst to Ocean Parkway. Now the exodus is to Deal, N.J., and Long Island communities such as Cedarhurst.

"We have lost some of our most substantial families," says Rabbi Abraham Hecht, director of Shaare Zion. Rabbi Hecht, like others among the community's elders, worries that if the trend continues, the Syrian Jewish population of Ocean Parkway may disappear in a decade.

'Survival of a Whole Culture'

Yesterday, however, such worries were not in evidence at the temple. The talk was of new members, new families—and new hopes.

Mr. Sutton, for example, recalled the efforts made by A. Bert Chabot, a community leader, who was instrumental, along with Stephen Shalom, formerly of Ocean Parkway and now of Kings Point, L. I., in arranging the marriage details.

"We're talking about the survival of a whole culture here," Mr. Sutton said, alluding to the fact that the major reason the Syrian women were marrying American Jews was that, for a variety of reasons, there are not enough eligible Jewish men left for them to marry in Syria.

About 10 men from Ocean Parkway's Jewish community have already been married to Syrians in a proxy ceremony, and two others, Charles Betesh of Brooklyn and Joseph Ackman of Baltimore flew to Damascus to be married in person.

These proxy marriages were legally accepted by the Syrian Government. That acceptance was critical since without it Damascus would not have permitted the emigration of the Jewish women. Some officials associated with Shaare Zion ventured the opinion last night that perhaps a few of the couples would undertake formal and full religious ceremonies in this country as well, largely for sentimental reasons.

Arranged Marriages a Tradition

The development is not new to the Jewish community in Syria. Arranged marriages have been traditional there and many of these marriages were performed by proxy, with parents and relatives standing in for their children.

Proxy marriages are not considered binding in Jewish law unless the rabbinate of both parties approves of the arrangement. And yesterday, officials of Shaare Zion indicated that, of course, these marriages most certainly had their blessings.

In addition, officials said, there was the likelihood that some couples would seek civil marriage licenses—although religious marriages are legally accepted in New York State as well as most states around the country.

The news of the weddings-to-be swirled around the synagogue yesterday. The word had also reached nearby Congregation Ahiezer, where Jews of Syrian descent also worship. Last night, after the sundown services, several men gathered in groups outside the houses of worship to talk about the situation.

The talk was not only about how the young men, most of them in their 20's and 30's, had volunteered for marriage, but how some had even signed letters of intent. A visitor asked a young man of the Shaare Zion Congregation why he had considered marrying one of the Syrian women, and what he expected of a bride-to-be whom he had never seen or spoken with.

"Marriage is marriage," was the reply, with a shrug.

Rabbi Hecht with the Lubavitcher Rebbe

Stones and Pebbles

When filling up a jar with stones, one has to insert each stone strategically to ensure that every inch of space is utilized. Large, bulky rocks are inserted first, followed by smaller pebbles that fill in the empty spaces.

I sometimes compared my work for the Rabbinic Council to a jar of rocks and pebbles. Several pressing issues, such as Kashrus and the eradication of intermarriage, claimed the dubious honor of mammoth rocks. They required boundless amounts of energy and attention for many long years, before they could be removed from the agenda. In the small spaces of time left at our disposal, smaller problems and responsibilities were poured in. These smaller, albeit significant, pebbles ascertained that each minute would be purposefully utilized.

Throughout the course of a Jewish year, there were numerous obligations that the Council or each individual rabbi was expected to carry out for the benefit of the community. As soon as one Yom Tov had departed, another one was inching its way around the corner. Thus, our work was a continuous string comprised of diverse services. It ranged from arranging the time and place for Kapparos before Yom Kippur, to the selling of Chometz prior to the Yom Tov Pesach.

Aside from the expected and much-anticipated holiday preparations, the Council offices were deluged with countless spoken and unspoken requests for assistance. Some difficulties were voiced, whereas others screamed wordlessly for rectification. I found myself answering these calls for help with varied remedies and treatments. Every situation called for a different set of methods that was tailor-made for its specific dimensions.

When the talking in my shul ballooned to unbearable proportions, I was forced to take action. I couldn't allow the inane chattering in the holiest community structure to continue unabated. My congregants had fallen into the habit of conversing with their friends and acquaintances during services, leading to a marked decrease in their respect for the sacred proceedings. Gentle rebuke or lectures would not succeed in stopping the raging epidemic, for its tentacles had spread with alarming speed throughout the entire congregation.

With my approval and encouragement, the Executive Committee of the Shaare Zion Congregation distributed a detailed letter about the changes that had to be implemented immediately. The blatant disrespect displayed by their talking in shul was elucidated in no uncertain terms.

"...All of us come to pray and hear the Sefer Torah. However, we have fallen into the habit of chatting with our friends and neighbors during the services. It has gotten so that the level of noise in the synagogue has reached epidemic proportions. Many people are turned off by our services.

"...We do not want our children to grow into the habit of using the synagogue primarily as a place to socialize, and secondly, a place to pray."

Several rules were clearly stated to remedy this problem, and they were enforced in due time. The Sefer Torah was read only when the sanctuary was completely silent. If there was the slightest murmur during the reading, the Baal Koreh was forced to pause until everyone quieted down. This practice was repeated several times, until the congregants understood that a shul is not the proper place for business, politics and everyday socializing.

Shabbos observance was another significant pebble rolling along the corridors of the Rabbinical Council. I was greatly bothered when some store owners unabashedly conducted business dealings long after the Shabbos Queen had swept along the Brooklyn streets. The sight of blazing lights in certain stores attacked the sensitivities of most community members, causing mutual dissent amongst the congregants.

September 28, 1986 was proclaimed as a day for "a mass meeting for Teshuvah". The public was asked to assemble in the Shaare Zion synagogue to discuss the incongruities evident in their lifestyle. Renowned speakers addressed the crowd with inspiring lectures about the beauty and significance of Shabbos observance. Tehillim was recited in unison, generating a warm feeling of unity and goodwill.

The metamorphosis didn't happen overnight, but with time we merited to witness a gradual return to stringent and unflinching Shabbos observance. My congregants learned to appreciate the gift of Shabbos and to value the elevated atmosphere it introduced in their lives.

These are only a few examples of the issues that consistently demanded our attention. The problems were dealt with on a communal basis for they were prevalent amongst most of my congregants. Conversely, the individual issues of certain community members called for specialized management. Some congregants required the services of a Bais Din, and after several years I succeeded in establishing one for our community.

In 1980, I organized and adjusted the foundation for a reliable and accepted Bais Din, which functioned under the title of the Sephardic Rabbinical Council. The organization catered to the needs of my Shaare Zion congregants in numerous areas. Since we never divulged the identities of those who turned to us or the cases we dealt with, many were unaware of the role we played. Some people felt abandoned and confused when they became entangled in a controversy. They didn't know about the halachic authorities who were willing to extend assistance in all situations.

Therefore, in September of 1987, I wrote a letter to the community at large, to apprise them of the services we were willing to offer. The Bais Din settled many business disputes between partners, between landlords and tenants, and any other money-related disagreements. We were also involved in reconciling serious familial issues between husband and wife, between parents and children and between two siblings.

The work was overwhelming and often frustrating, but the satisfaction of successfully circumventing a storm of feuds was well-worth the price. At day's end, the dayanim were exhausted but they exulted in the knowledge that they had settled disputes in accordance with the dictates of the Torah.

Between my responsibilities as the vice-president of the Rabbinical Council, my obligations to the Shaare Zion congregation and the work engendered by the newly-established Bais Din, I was running a marathon. My path was generously strewn with obstacles, yet fulfillment and satisfaction always followed close behind. As soon as I crossed the finish line of one project, a fresh path was revealed, challenging me on to greater heights.

While I was dealing with problems in the Sephardic community, there were several instances when my attention was required in pressing worldwide issues. I was once asked to deal with the United Nations on a matter which had never been discussed in its hallowed corridors. At the behest of the Lubavitcher Rebbe zt"l, I tried to organize an opportunity to speak before the nations of the world. The Rebbe asked me to discuss the Seven Noahide Laws, the Sheva Mitzvos Bnei Noach, in the United Nations. Upon hearing the idea, I was beset by apprehension. Why should the ambassadors be willing to hear about this topic? Would it be possible to get permission for this unprecedented venture?

Despite my misgivings, I started exploring my options. A

meeting was arranged with Ambassador Okun, the U.S.A. Ambassador to the United Nations and his staff to discuss my suggestion. The matter was viewed and reviewed, until a decision was reached. Although I would be unable to deliver my request personally at the United Nations, permission was granted for a different approach. The Rebbe's remarks would be printed on the letterhead of the American embassy and placed on every desk in the United Nations. Thus, the ambassadors from various countries would be informed that the American government approves of the contents and they would subsequently be voted on.

I was elated at my success in a mission which had appeared close to impossible. For technical reasons, the Rebbe's remarks were never distributed in the U.N., although the sought-after approval had been received. The hours of thought and preparation that were invested in this undertaking were mere grains of sand in the large hourglass of my life as a Rabbi.

The years I spent in the Sephardic community were full of large rocks and little pebbles. Each individual stone sparkled with multi-hued beauty after it was carefully polished and shined. Strung together on the chains of time, these difficulties and achievements formed an awesome string of valuable gems. The shimmering diamonds attest to siyata dishmaya, hard work, and the constant support of a faithful companion.

Lillian a"h, my wife and companion for fifty-nine years, has helped me string those gems into a chain of achievement. Her supportive, loyal presence allowed me to grow in ways which would have been impossible without her assistance. Looking back upon the past few decades, I can only thank Hashem for the priceless gift he has granted to me. Now that she has ascended to a higher world, I am certain that she continues to pray on behalf of her children and family, who strive to emulate her ways.

'Proxy' Syrian Brides Meet Their Grooms in New York

"I was extremely nervous," Edward Gindi said last night. "I really didn't know what to expect." Mr. Gindi's nervousness was understandable. He had gone to John F. Kennedy International Airport to meet—for the first time—Amlia Halabi, the woman to whom he was married by proxy in Syria.

They were among a dozen couples who were united yesterday after having been married in the unusual proxy ceremony after months of secret discussions between the Carter Administration and the Government of President Hafez al-Assad of Syria.

"When I saw her, my nervousness disappeared immediately," Mr. Gindi said. "She is very beautiful and I hope things work out between us."

"Oh, they surely will," Miss Halabi confidently interjected in Arabic, a language that Mr. Gindi does not understand. An interpreter had to translate the words into English, which Miss Halabi does not speak.

Miss Halabi was one of 12 Syrian Jewish women who flew into New York City last night from Damascus, and Mr. Gindi was one of a dozen Jews of Syrian descent who live in the Ocean Parkway area of Brooklyn who had agreed to marry the women by proxy. President Assad had insisted that the women first find husbands in this country before they would be permitted to emigrate.

Bachelors Needed

There is increasing concern among Syria's 5,100 Jews about finding eligible bachelors to marry the 500 or so unmarried women of the community. According to Syrian Jewish leaders, the problem has arisen because most single Jewish men have been able to slip out of the country and those who remain appear to be unwilling to marry because they want to be able to leave on short notice, unencumbered by a family.

So many men have left Syria, or plan to do so, because Jews there in recent years have had to live with discriminatory rules restricting their travel and their freedom to sell property. Last January, President Assad relaxed some of these restrictions but he still refused to let Jews to emigrate—largely because of fear that they would travel to neighboring Israel.

But the dozen Syrian brides who arrived in New York last night did so as a result of Washington's diplomacy—and the efforts of the Syrian Jewish community along Brooklyn's Ocean Parkway, a tree-lined, largely residential area that has the single largest concentration of the 40,000 Jews of Syrian origin in this country, nearly 25,000.

Syrian customs are followed there and Arabic is widely spoken—even though there are many young men, like Mr. Gindi, who do not speak the language. So, according to Representative Stephen J. Solarz, Democrat of Brooklyn who was involved in the complicated negotiations, Syrian Jewish leaders specifically asked that the women be permitted to emigrate to the Brooklyn neighborhood.

Last night, Mr. Solarz was among dozens of relatives of bridegrooms and other members of the Syrian Jewish community who waited at the airport for the brides.

Bridegrooms Seemed Anxious

Mr. Gindi and Jeffrey Sholom seemed visibly anxious. Some chewed on their fingernails; others paced.

At 8:05 P.M., Air France Flight 17 from Paris arrived, and about 25 minutes after that the men got to see the women they had agreed to marry.

Most of the dozen women wore colorful skirts. Others wore jeans. All carried shopping bags. And all were smiling and waving happily, even though none had met the bridegrooms, or even seen photographs of them.

The new arrivals were led to a news conference, where Brooklyn Syrian Jews competed with reporters and photographers for a view of the women.

"We are very thankful to be here," Tira Souid, who acted as spokesman for the women, said, as members of her new community applauded robustly. "We are very, very thankful."

The man who had married her by proxy, Mr. Sholom, stood along with his colleagues behind the women. Asked if he was nervous, he replied, "Of course," as Miss Souid turned around and beamed at him.

Rabbi Abraham Hecht, the spiritual leader of the Shaare Zion Congregation of Ocean Parkway and ont of those chiefly instrumental in bringing about the brides arrival, smiled, too, as did Steven Shalom, an investment banker, who had arranged for the details of the ceremonies in Syria.

Rabbi Hecht said the women would be housed with families in Brooklyn. He said that although under Jewish tradition proxy marriages are accepted, under New York State law the couples would first have to obtain a civil marriage license. Only after that, could a Jewish religious marriage be performed.

Meanwhile, the young men and women will begin a period of courtship.

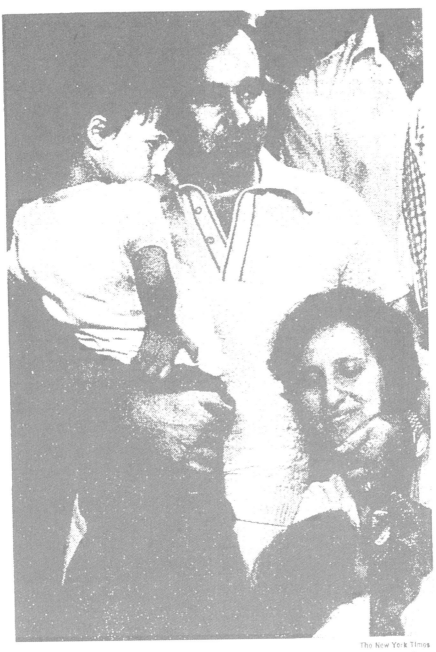

The New York Times

Sarah Halwani, a widow with three children, is embraced by her brother, after arriving from Syria with 12 Syrian brides.

The New York Times/Marilynn K. Yee

FIRST MEETING: Representative Stephen J. Solarz, left foreground, and Rabbi Abraham Hecht, officiate at welcoming ceremony last night at Kennedy International Airport for 12 Syrian Jewish brides, center, who arrived last night to meet American husbands by proxy marriage for the first time. Page B14.

The Rabbi in Congress

My efforts on behalf of the community sometimes brought me to the highest echelons of American society. At times, my gestures of goodwill were met with appreciation and genuine gratitude, as is evidenced in a letter I received from Congressman Solarz. On impulse, I had decided to treat him to some hand-baked shmurah matzos in honor of the upcoming holiday. His effusive thanks convinced me that the effort had been well-invested.

"I can't begin to tell you how much I appreciated the hand-baked matzos which you sent me for the Passover holiday," Solarz wrote several days after Pesach.

"I thought you would like to know that my wife and I were privileged to have Vice President and Mrs. Mondale as our guests for the first night of the Seder at our home in Virginia, and we used the matzo you had sent us for the occasion.

"I told the Vice President, by the way, that he would now know, if nothing else, that the conflict between Israel and Egypt didn't begin thirty years ago!"

Another example of the friendly relationship I forged with the officials I dealt with is the farewell letter I received from Michael Lewin. Mike was the executive assistant of Congressmen Solarz for eight years, and we therefore had plenty of opportunities to work together. Before he left his position, Mike wrote a few words in parting, and added a postscript that has remained engraved in my mind.

"Thanks, you're my favorite Rabbi!"

These simple words, added on the spur of the moment as a postscript to a beautiful letter, are the most genuine tokens of friendship and camaraderie.

Aside from the informal connections I forged with several government officials, I was privileged to attend several sessions at the Senate and at the House of Representatives. At these occasions, my status was not that of a mere spectator, for I was asked to introduce these meetings with a short prayer. I accepted the responsibility with anticipation tinged with apprehension. Speaking in government circles was not something I had prepared myself for upon accepting my position as Rabbi of the Sephardic community.

Being an observant Jew and a loyal American, I tried to combine and include all facets of my existence in the preliminary speeches I was asked to deliver. April 25, 1966 marked the date of my first appearance in the Senate. I proclaimed the words of my prayer with pride and confidence before the staid and respected government officials. Much thought had been invested in the exact wording of the prayer, and I hoped that they would reach the intended target.

"*Avinu b'shamayim..*" I started, in Hebrew. As I proudly enunciated each word, I wondered whether the walls of the Senate had ever merited hearing the syllables of Loshon Hakodesh. Imbued with a sense of purpose, I proceeded to elucidate my views, based on the teachings of the Torah. After the first introductory sentence, I spoke in English, for the convenience of my American audience.

"Bless this august assembly and their families. May they be granted peace of mind, serenity and spirit, and inner tranquility predicated upon faith and trust in the Creator. May those who occupy themselves with the affairs of our country always faith-

*fully seek Your guidance in pursuing its welfare, its advance-
ment, its growth and security."*

I glanced at the faces of the Senators and was pleased to note
their attentive and interested expressions. The inclusion of Hashem in the workings of the government cast a different light on
their laudable occupation. After expounding on our reliance on
Hashem for the continued success of the American existence, I
directly translated some of the lines said by the Navi Yeshaya.
The excerpt from his prophecy was a prayer begging Hashem to
bring an end to pain and suffering.

Upon concluding, I once again reminded the assemblage
what their success really depended on.

"We pray to the Ruler of the universe," I announced, *"that
His blessing continue to be bestowed on all inhabitants of our
country, that fears and dangers, prejudice and malice be removed from its borders, and that all its citizens, regardless of
race, color, or creed, will know the joys of prosperity, tranquility, and peace. Amen."*

Following my introductory prayer, matters proceeded regularly as the senators dealt with the day-to-day business involved
in running the government. After delivering the preliminary
greeting, I immensely enjoyed my role as spectator in such grandiose and official surroundings. I also attended a grand reception following the session in Congress, which was comprised of
strictly kosher food and drinks as it was catered by members of
my community. Their thoughtful adjustments for my benefit
were greatly appreciated for it precluded an extremely uncomfortable situation. At the reception, Senator Monlyhan congratulated me on my successful remarks.

"Your words were piped into the offices of countless Congressmen, Rabbi Hecht. My wife immensely enjoyed it and wishes to convey her thanks for your thought-provoking speech."

Approximately two years later, I repeated a similar prayer at the beginning of a session in the House of Representatives. Once again, I started in Hebrew, proudly broadcasting my Jewish roots.

> *"Ruler of the universe, we express our deep gratitude to you, for the miracle of civilization we call America. The ideals of liberty, equality and personal freedom, the bedrocks of our society, serve today to millions throughout the world as the most desirable virtues of government.*
>
> *"...We pray that You will guide and direct these Members of Congress, to legislate fearlessly in the spirit of truth and justice; to remove the scourges of crime and violence threatening to destroy the fabric of our national security; to pursue the goals of universal peace with honor; to effectuate a conciliation between East and West; to assist the needy and oppressed at home and abroad; and to recognize the valid claims of the Jewish State for support — moral and material."*

I concluded with a verse from Tehillim, saying, *"In the words of the Psalmist we pray, 'May He who made heaven and earth, bless you from Zion.' Amen."*

As I had done during my other visits to the Senate and the House, I tried to infuse the esteemed Congressmen with an understanding and appreciation of the One who controls their every move. These government officials were situated at the peak of their respective careers, but they were still firmly in the hands of their Creator. If their understanding of this concept was subject to the slightest improvement, I would consider this mission successful.

I was privileged to offer preliminary remarks a total of four times; twice in the Senate and twice in the House of Representatives. At each occasion, I tried to infuse my words with the conviction and belief that is a prerequisite for anyone situated in a position of power. In December of 1975, Congressman Stephen

J. Solarz complimented me on the speech I had just given, expressing his opinion in a warm, friendly letter.

"It was really good to have you with us here in Washington a short while ago," Solarz wrote. "I've gotten so many favorable comments from my colleagues on your prayer that I think we could even elect you, if you're interested, as the permanent Rabbi of the House, when we convene next year."

He enclosed a copy of the Congressional Record, which I added to the others that I had accumulated over the years. I carefully stored the official documentation of my visits in Congress. The records proudly bear my prayers on behalf of America; a democratic nation which carries the responsibility of true democracy on its broad shoulders.

Incidentally, my prayers with the Hebrew words were printed in the Congressional Record, which records all the events of each day in the Record.

On two occasions, additional remarks made by friendly Congressmen and Senators, were included in the Record.

Each event was followed by a Kosher dinner attended by several Congressmen and Senators.

This does not make the end of my book as I would like it to be continued with the help of G-d for many more years to come, Amen.

INDEX TO PICTURES